CONTENTS AT A GLANCE

CREATING KILLER INTERACTIVE WEB SITES

Library of Congress Catalog Number: 96-70861
ISBN: 1-56830-373-4

Printed in the United States of America 1 2 3 4 5 6 7 8 9 0

WARNING AND DISCLAIMER

This book is sold as is, without warranty of any kind, either express or implied. While every precaution has been taken in the preparation of this book, the authors and Hayden Books assume no responsibility for errors or omissions. Neither is any liability assumed for damages resulting from the use of the information or instructions contained herein. It is further stated that the publisher and authors are not responsible for any damage or loss to your data or your equipment that results directly or indirectly from your use of this book.

Trademark Acknowledgments: All terms mentioned in this book that are known to be trademarks or services marks have been appropriately capitalized. Hayden Books cannot attest to the accuracy of this information. Use of a term in this book should not be regarded as affecting the validity of any trademark or service mark.

HAYDEN BOOKS

President
Richard Swadley

Associate Publisher
John Pierce

Publishing Manager
Laurie Petrycki

Managing Editor
Lisa Wilson

Acquisitions Editor
Michelle Reed

Product Development Specialist
Steve Mulder

Copy/Production Editor
Kevin Laseau

Publishing Coordinator
Karen Williams

Cover and Book Designer
Planet Design Company and
Adjacency

Manufacturing Coordinator
Brook Farling

Production Team Supervisors
Laurie Casey and Joe Millay

Production Team
Diana Groth, Linda Knose,
Malinda Kuhn, Scott Tullis,
Megan Wade

Indexer
Chris Wilcox

ABOUT THE COMPANY

Adjacency (`http://www.adj.com`) is a full-service new media design firm based in San Francisco. The company specializes in corporate web site strategy development, conceptualization, design, content development, production, programming, hosting and ongoing support, and expansion.

Founded in early 1995, Adjacency's first clients were Patagonia of Ventura, CA, and Specialized Bicycle Components of Morgan Hill, CA. Adjacency continues to serve those companies and more, including Land Rover, Rollerblade, Motorola, Kemper Funds, Burns Philp Foods, Lufthansa, Boehringer Ingelheim, Pixar, and Powerfood.

Adjacency's mission is to strive to provide some of the best consumer brands on the planet with some of the best sites on the World Wide Web. Period.

ABOUT THE AUTHORS

Andrew Sather

Trained in graphic design, creative writing, and art history, Andrew Sather believes that good design combined with moments of creative epiphany, though insufficient to save the planet, makes it a much more pleasant place to be. Born, raised, and schooled in Madison, WI, Andrew recently moved to San Francisco. Andrew serves as Adjacency's Creative Director and CEO.

Ardith Ibañez

Ardith Ibañez joined the *Creating Killer Interactive Web Sites* team backed by her experiences as a co-author of *HTML Web Magic*, a senior designer for Macromedia's award-winning web site, and co-founder and creative director of Akimbo Design (`http://www.akimbodesign.com/`).

Bernie DeChant

Bernie DeChant is Adjacency's art director. A Racine, WI native, Bernie now lives on top of San Francisco's Portrero Hill. Between his many projects, he manages to find time to hammer on the piano and bike the mountains around the Bay Area. Bernie drifted around between several design and advertising firms before joining Adjacency.

Pascal

Hailing from Mobile, AL, Pascal now lives in the Mission in San Francisco, following brief stops in Hattiesburg, MS, Swansea, Wales, and Madison, WI. Each morning he wakes up wondering whether he is a designer or a programmer.

Pascal, a long-time vegetarian, joined Adjacency after working on Oscar Mayer's web site. He thinks bikes are cooler than hot dogs.

DEDICATION

For Manzi, Bud, Luke, Erika, and Kathryn.

For all the college students with overdue copies of *Graphis* and *Communication Arts* on their bookshelves.

For all the people with the courage and creativity to bust out and do their own thing for their own reasons.

And perhaps most importantly for all the clients who, we think, made the right choice.

- Andrew

To Mom and Andy, Mary Jo, Lee, Eddie, Brian, Janette, Joann, Bobby, and all their significant others, to my father and Jackie and Mimi, to Eddie and Karl Moore for teaching me the fundamentals painting billboards in basements and the outfields, and to all the people in the SC Johnson Wax Creative Department for giving me my first break. Finally, to all my friends and loved ones who've had to deal with me during the countless 100 hour+ weeks put into that fun thing known as starting a business, this is for you.

- Bernie

To my loving husband and most righteous dude, Ben, who took such good care of me, feeding me delicious meals, cleaning the apartment, building the flowerboxes for our windows, and making sure I went outside every so often. Who said there's such a thing as a starving artist?

To our parents, Dan, Gloria, Helen, and Gerry for supporting me even though they don't really understand what the heck I'm doing. To Nanay Lina, my grandmother, for staying in the United States to see me finish my second book, start my own business, and get married. She's so cool.

- Ardith

25% of this book is dedicated to my mama.

- Pascal

ACKNOWLEDGMENTS

Everybody at Adjacency could have written this book. They all know the score. They've been living, breathing, and dreaming killer web sites since before the term was popularized. It has been the greatest honor for all of us to work with the Adjacency team past and present: Anton, Matt, Matia, Carlo, Joe, Sich, Kathryn, Zo, Charlie, Kristen, Andy, Ron, Greg, Arturo, Jen, Frost, Dan, Ramsey, Stefan, Stein, Don, Andi, Marge, the other Andrew, Godwin, Brett, Jake, Streeter, Jason, Karen, Vientienne, and the venerable Vincent Rose.

This book would not have been created without the generosity and vision of certain key people from the organization formerly known as NeXT including, but not limited to, Katherine Singson, Brandon Greimann, Helen Casabona, Dianna Vallance, and Steve Jobs.

Much thanks and adoration to Planet Design Company's Martha "Mothra" Graettinger, Kevin "Boom-Boom" Wade, Dana Lytle, and John Besmer, who proved to us that world class design is not geographically dependent and that great designers are rock stars, too.

Ardith would like to thank the amazing web designers at Macromedia: Nat, Jason, Jorge, and honorary team members, Christine and Elliot, who inspire her ceaselessy and transformed her into the web designing maniac she is today.

Thanks to all our friends and family members who understood when we didn't call or write, when we showed up late or forgot about appointments, when we fell asleep in the middle of conversations, or rescheduled get-togethers 10,000 times because of writing this "killer" book.

And mentors! Most of us would be working for the man without the guidance, wisdom, and whip-cracking of people such as John Rieben, Philip Hamilton, Jim Escalante, and Dennis Miller. And every young writer wants to be like Rebecca Lee when they grow up; and every business person wants to be like Brad Keywell and Erik Lefkofsky.

Without our fabulous clients, there would be no web sites about which to write. We have been unbelievably fortunate for such a great group of clients. Thanks to Ed Schmultz, Chris Murphy, Chris Marchand, Randy Saba, Michael Neu, Richard Taylor, Pat Allen, Bill Jackoboice, Dave Dulfer, Tom Dwyer, Bill Boland, Peter Sapienza, Lori Ipsen, Jen Pagnini, Deb Autrey, Maureen O'Neill, Rick Carlson, Peter Haag, Ann Endrusick, Kim Myers, Tim "T-Money" Tumbleson, Nancy Comerford, Kerry May, Diane Dreis, Michael Faltinowski, David Valentine, Tony Costa, John Partridge, Kim Gore, Wilbur Swan, Chris DeVore, Oliver Sellnick, Susan Vaughan, Jane McCroary, Garrett Lai, Mary Jo Shavitz, Ken Raley, Karen McRoberts, Jennifer Rydzewski, Irene

Yeh, Paul Fuegner, Patricia Saraceni, Michael Scott, Patty Ozaki, Bryan Brosamle, Kim Koss, John Mickelson, Mike Bisner, Karyn Silva, and Mike Adams.

Thanks to Michelle Reed and Kevin Laseau of Hayden Books and all the other editors and publishers who, though really nice people, all but disappear amid Michelle's radiance. Thanks to Steve Mulder. We miss you Steve!

Lastly, we'd like to thank David "High Five" Siegel for making people care about and understand web design, and of course, for creating the "Killer" book series.

HAYDEN BOOKS

The staff of Hayden Books is committed to bringing you the best computer books. What our readers think of Hayden is important to our ability to serve our customers. If you have any comments, no matter how great or how small, we'd appreciate your taking the time to send us a note.

You can reach Hayden Books at the following:

Hayden Books
201 West 103rd Street
Indianapolis, IN 46290
317-581-3833

Email addresses:

| America Online: | Hayden Bks |
| Internet: | hayden@hayden.com |

Visit the Hayden Books Web site at `http://www.hayden.com`

And of course, visit the *Creating Killer Interactive Web Sites* book site at `http://www.adj.com/killer`

| Email Adjacency: | killer@adj.com |

TABLE OF CONTENTS

WHY READ THIS BOOK?

By reading this book, you learn a project-proven process for building engaging, elegant, and powerful web sites. Although the case studies in this book discuss corporate web sites, you can adapt the design and strategy concepts to your own web sites. All web sites, corporate or otherwise, tell a story and convey information. They share common issues in interface design, as well as information design and organization. Ultimately, all web sites compete for viewers with every other web site. Corporate site design is one the fastest-evolving, most innovative areas of web site design due to the steep competition among clients and design firms.

We hope you enjoy our case studies that illustrate how Adjacency has developed corporate web sites for Specialized®, Land Rover®, North America, Lufthansa®, Motorola®, Rollerblade®, and Patagonia®, just to name a few. By reading this book, you learn:

◆ **How to combine good graphic design sensibilities, visual branding strategies, and web technology.** Learn how to create sites that engage, entertain, and inform users.

◆ **How to create sites that visually live up to your content.** The majority of web sites are stronger on the content side than design and navigation. Learn how to create a well-rounded web site that draws from the best of all three areas.

◆ **How to look at your message, organize your information better, and display it more boldly and more interactively.** Learn how to create compelling features that motivates your users to interact in a meaningful way with your information.

WHO SHOULD USE THIS BOOK

Anyone who is interested in and who creates work for the World Wide Web can use this book including:

◆ Graphic designers
◆ Programmers
◆ Anyone faced with a decision of building a web site
◆ Anyone with an affiliation to or responsibility for a (consumer) brand

We set up *Creating Killer Interactive Web Sites* in such a way that the different players in the development process can take steps to improve how they plan, organize, manage, execute, and promote a web site. We wrote and designed this book to present the bigger picture behind web site development to address the necessity for better, interdisciplinary approaches to web design.

The running narrative text throughout the book walks you through the entire process, while case studies and sidebars give you valuable examples of implementation and detailed directions.

The case studies illustrate our experiences with our clients and provide real-world scenarios of how we've applied the theories and techniques we discuss. The sidebars provide useful details and tools for specific techniques, such as preparing graphics for the web, building interactive features, and making your site at once more dynamic and more manageable. We have also created a companion web site at `http://www.adj.com/killer` to provide valuable downloadable resources and online examples related to topics and techniques discussed here on paper.

We sincerely hope this book enlightens, educates, and inspires you.

INTRODUCTION

THE BOOM OF THE WORLD WIDE WEB

Long gone are the days of "text-only" information on web pages with drab gray backgrounds. With graphics, sound, and animation, the World Wide Web now possesses the potential to be highly dynamic and interactive. People can now design interfaces as strong and compelling as the actual content of their sites.

THE EVOLUTION OF WEB PAGE DESIGN

When Tim Berners-Lee first envisioned the medium that would become the World Wide Web in a particle physics laboratory in Switzerland, he had no idea what a monster would be born of his hands. He had only set out to solve a simple problem in communication among scientists.

Berners-Lee, himself a scientist, recognized that scientists and educators could benefit greatly if they had a means to more easily distribute information—particularly research papers. He recognized that due to the great volume of work being produced, there needed to be a way of structuring that information so that scientists could more readily get at the information they needed. And he recognized that because scientists were using a wide variety of computer platforms, there needed to be some standard means of structuring that information so that anyone with any computer could access it.

To solve this problem, he created HTML—the HyperText Markup Language. It was meant to be a simple set of tools to format information in a logical manner and to facilitate the creation of links between related bits of information.

What Berners-Lee perhaps did not recognize was that many people in many other fields were facing the same problems as scientists—and they rapidly began turning to HTML as their solution, as well. Fortunately, Berners-Lee had designed HTML to be easy to learn, so people in non-technical professions were capable of producing pages. The web began to grow—rapidly.

A few short years later, the web was rivaling email as the most popular use of the Internet. People from all walks of life were browsing and creating web pages. Some of them, of course, were designers.

Being accustomed to presenting information in graphically rich ways, using huge type, four-color photography, and precision layouts, many designers shunned the web at first, choosing to remain in the familiar realm of print. Those who did move to the new medium usually resigned themselves to living within the prescribed limits of HTML, using <H1> to create large type and sprinkling their text with the occasional inline GIF or JPEG, all on default gray backgrounds. Some of the more innovative designers produced interesting solutions to design problems using onscreen type alone. But for most designers, this wasn't enough to satisfy them.

For many of them, Netscape was the savior they had been waiting for. Bringing such innovations as the `<FONT SIZE>` attribute, background colors and images, borderless tables, and the venerable `<BLINK>` tag, Netscape recognized that HTML needed to be extended to meet people's need for more control over the aesthetic presentation of information. Controversial as it was to many old-timers, the strategy was wildly successful. Netscape rapidly became the most widely used browser, and designers started coming to the web in droves.

Even its present state, with further extensions from Netscape, Microsoft, and others, HTML is far from ideal as a method of executing successful design solutions. The web, as always, is rapidly changing; new means of reaching design goals appear on the horizon every day.

Today, fast-growing web technology and decreasing hardware and software prices make it easier for people across the world to view and create web pages. *Internet service providers*, *web browsers*, and HTML have increasingly found their way into common vernacular. Moms, dads, 7-year-olds, college students, big business, small business—more and more people are getting connected.

NEW ATTITUDE TOWARDS WEB DESIGN

Although the widespread information exchange made possible by the web reaps positive results, the boom in this industry also involves serious repercussions. "Everybody's doing it." But it's time for everybody to start doing it right. The immediacy of the web makes it too easy for people to upload their work quickly without careful consideration. We must stop, address the medium, and figure out why people would use a web site. We must find better ways to organize information to engage users.

We must design web sites as applications, not just as collections of individual web pages. Web sites must earn their bandwidth by addressing a true need and must use the inherent strengths of the medium to organize and disseminate information and enable people to interact with information in meaningful, customizable, at times, spontaneous ways. We must consistently remind ourselves that real people go to web sites seeking information to deal with real-world issues or problems.

We also have a responsibility of designing sites that look great and are easy to use. In order to achieve this balance, a more holistic, interdisciplinary approach to web design must be assumed. Designers must acquire a knowledge of the technical side of the development process and programmers, the aesthetic. Designers must challenge programmers to accommodate new, more sophisticated, unexpected ways of displaying and organizing information online and programmers must encourage designers to think about design in more techno-savvy, fluid, interactive and functional terms. Design alone will not save the web; nor will technology. Those two disciplines married with elements of architecture, art and music, communications, publishing, interior and environmental design, psychology and sociology, advertising, and marketing will inform the most effective and refreshing, paradigm-exploding web design to come. Everyone's talking about thinking outside of the box. Go further. Deny the existence of the box and embrace the infinite possibilities of a medium as organic as the breed that built it.

OVERVIEW OF ADJACENCY'S PROCESS

Creating Killer Interactive Web Sites involves steps that weave the concepts discussed earlier with a certain design and development methodology. This book dedicates a chapter to each of the six steps of Adjacency's process. In such a nonlinear medium as the web, planning, organization, execution, and follow-through play key roles in creating a successful web site.

- ◆ **Chapter 1: Evaluating the Brand** This chapter helps you establish goals and objectives for your web site by helping you determine what exactly it is you are trying to promote or express.
- ◆ **Chapter 2: Developing Site Strategy and Structure** This chapter helps you understand your target audience(s) in order to plan an effective site architecture.
- ◆ **Chapter 3: Designing Web Site Aesthetics** This chapter walks you through the steps of designing an effective user interface for your web site.
- ◆ **Chapter 4: Designing and Building Interactivity** This chapter helps you come up with interactive features that accomplish your objectives as well as enhance your web site by discussing the technology that makes interactivity possible.
- ◆ **Chapter 5: Promoting Your Web Site** This chapter helps you reach and lure your web site audience.
- ◆ **Chapter 6: Maintaining Your Web Site** This chapter helps you secure steady and perhaps increased traffic to your site.

Don't just read the book...visit the web site! Adjacency has created a companion web site to serve as a complementary resource to this book. It can be visited at:

`http://www.adj.com/killer`

There you'll find links to all the sites mentioned in this book, online demonstrations of many of the principles we discuss, technical short cuts and links to great shareware, and perhaps most importantly, killer source code that's yours for the taking. You'll also find a discussion forum featuring bi-weekly chat sessions with the authors. Plus, enter your favorite sites in Adjacency's *Creating Killer Interactive Web Sites* contest.

CHAPTER 1

BEFORE PLANNING THE STRUCTURE AND DESIGNING THE INTERFACE OF A WEB SITE, YOU MUST

FIRST UNDERSTAND THE IDENTITY OF THE PRODUCT YOU WANT TO PORTRAY AND PROMOTE.

THE NOTION OF A "PRODUCT" REPRESENTS THE SUBJECT MATTER OF YOUR WEB SITE REGARD-

LESS OF WHETHER OR NOT IT IS A TANGIBLE, CONSUMER GOOD. A PRODUCT CAN MANIFEST

IN THE FORM OF A SERVICE,

EVENT, OR SIMPLY AN IDEA.

EVALUATING
THE BRAND

DISTILLING YOUR CLIENT'S BRAND AND CORPORATE IDENTITY

Understanding a brand is indeed a major endeavor. The following sidebar "What Is a Brand?" guides you through the first steps in understanding your client's brand and corporate identity. We also discuss specific areas and issues you should consider and look out for in evaluating your client company. We tell you how to work with a client's existing corporate identity materials to get a handle on the essence of the company. Take advantage of the resources readily available to you. Very often, a company will already have print or broadcast materials that define their brand in the media.

WHAT IS A BRAND?

Until recently, a problem with many big-name corporate web sites was that they were concerned with products and not brands. People expect comprehensive product information from a medium so exhaustive as the web, but such material should be integrated into sites as thoroughly and unassumingly as possible. Anyone can build a web site about products…but brands are a bit trickier.

A brand is a combination of a lot of things. It's public perception and history of the product and the company that makes and markets it. It's the product name. Branding is the product's visual identity and packaging. It's the consumers' association between the product and things such as quality, style, or functionality.

Rollerblade, for example, is more than a product or a company. Consumers go so far as to confuse the company and the product with the sport. The name Rollerblade evokes different things for different people, but it generally represents mobility, activity, freedom, freshness, and fun. Rollerblade's history as the developer of an entirely new sport and sports equipment category blends with peoples' impressions of the brand as an embodiment of something new and adventurous. This creates a value that is far more than a sum of the technology and design of the products combined with its market share. It's the sort of value that drives other companies to pay Rollerblade handsome sums to license the Rollerblade name so they can make and sell things such as tennis shoes and sunglasses under the Rollerblade brand name.

Branding is the trust and greater identification that consumers have in one product or company over others. In many ways, a brand represents to consumers a collection of traits or values those people aspire to or respect. The best brands are inseparable from the products they represent, but at the same time they are portable to other product categories. When Land Rover introduced a clothing line, for instance, most consumers already familiar with the company's vehicles knew what to expect—rugged, purposeful clothing to complement and support the outdoor lifestyle.

Web sites that serve not only the products a company offers but ultimately the brand behind them are essential. Web sites that don't are disposable.

By building a site that is more than a repurposed online product catalog, you are creating a valuable interactive property that logically and gracefully accommodates a company's future product offerings and advertising messages. By seeking a brand's values, a company's soul, and embodying and celebrating it online, you create a solid foundation that enables you to grow your client's online presence as the Internet grows and evolves.

The web is an amazing medium for brands because you can accomplish the long-term goal of brand exposure while at the same time combining elements of direct marketing, customer support, market research, and sales. An effective web site speaks to all dimensions of a brand without confusing the consumer.

REVIEW ALL EXISTING CORPORATE IDENTITY MATERIALS

In order to understand the brand, you must first analyze all existing corporate identity materials—print collateral, broadcast spots, usage manuals, even the company's retail presence. Before a company approaches you with plans to create a web site, more often than not, they already have something tangible that defines and communicates their image to the general public—whether it is simply a logotype or a full blown advertising campaign.

A company's logo, letterhead, packaging, and business cards all contribute to a brand image that the web site would acknowledge and in some way support. Web sites serve as the newest ingredient in companies' constantly evolving marketing recipe. They should enhance, yet reinforce, the flavor of the entire corporate identity. The corporate communications suite as a whole needs to convey a strong, unified message. If you were to place all of the company's advertising and design pieces in a row, you would want the group to fit (see Figure 1.1).

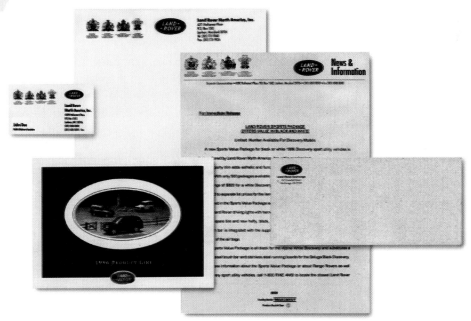

Figure 1.1
Land Rover's brand identity is consistently represented in their stationery and print collateral

The following are a few questions to ask yourself and your client in order to understand the brand better. You should also refer to the branding sidebar earlier in this chapter.

◆ What is the client company's voice?

You cannot communicate with somebody without assuming a manner of speech or writing style. Companies are like people. As a consumer, you know what you think a brand should "sound" like. Honda is witty and informal. Lexus is stately and serious. When you read an advertisement, watch a television commercial, or visit the web site of a brand you're familiar with, you should be able to get a feeling for whether or not the style fits. It's your job as a site's developer or as a client to try to make sure your site speaks with your company's voice lest your site become a mouthpiece for a brand ventriloquist.

◆ Does the client already have an existing branding system? Or, does it simply have a disparate set of images tied together with a logo? Will you have to create images from scratch?

Smart companies tend to canonize certain aspects of and approaches to most elements of a brand's portrayal. You must determine if any design elements serve as visual cues for the brand from medium to medium. Logo treatment and placement, use of tag lines or headlines, image types and their placement and manipulation, key colors, and typography can all be part of such a system. Think of it as corporate identity, design standards, and their practice all combined.

◆ How does the company use photographic material?

It's worth belaboring this point a little. Many web sites are created by people who assume you must use photos in limited, web-friendly ways: Small images, sometimes silhouetted, but usually cropped into tidy little rectangles. Web conventions were meant to be innovated out of existence. Take some leads from the more ambitious image use you may find in a company's print and broadcast work. As you read on, you may be surprised by some of the unexpected things you can do on a web site with a few good photos.

◆ What kind of typography fits the brand?

Every company has favorite typefaces. Every brand also has a range of typeface styles that, when used correctly and smartly, are tolerated and really drive messages home. Pay attention to type. Just because Times and Courier have traditionally been the most popular hypertext fonts by default, that doesn't mean you shouldn't use headlines and subheads created as GIF images to fight the oppressively bland look of bit-mapped, black 12-point Times.

◆ Are there any existing visual guidelines with which you must design the web site?

You will find, especially when developing sites for divisions or subsidiaries of large corporations, that many organizations have codified web site design standards. Similarly, nearly all companies have corporate usage manuals to ensure proper use of their visual identity. You must factor such predetermined creative direction into your understanding of the appropriate look and feel for a site.

◆ In what other mediums do consumers see the brand?

Does your company advertise on TV predominantly or print? Full color magazines? Black-and-white newspaper ads? Direct marketing? Annoying dinner-time unsolicited phone calls by people who can't properly pronounce your name? Banners at trade shows and public events? On the side of a Formula One car? By understanding how and where consumers receive your company's branding messages and by trying to put yourself in their shoes, you can make more sound instinctive and strategic decisions when designing your web site, when creating the structure of the site, and when you promote it. This understanding helps make your web site's brand affiliation as recognizable as possible and further message retention among visitors.

◆ What kind of expectations do consumers have based on the most popular representations of the brand? What kind of feel? What kind of pace? What kind of genre?

Perhaps you have a witty, cynical brand on your hands that deserves a sarcastic site that spoofs somebody else. Or maybe consumers are familiar with the company through serious, authoritative TV commercials that represent the height of decorum. Such a company may best be served by an elegant but informative web site with few surprises. Other sites may feel like games, communities, adventures/stories, publications, places, or combinations of those ideas and more.

◆ What image do consumers have of the brand? Is it consistent with the company's goals?

Web sites, as with all mediums, are sometimes enlisted to not only reinforce a brand's messages but also to counter or refute consumer misconceptions. Nearly every company has

work to do in this area and most of them know it. It's important to know what you're up against.

Working with existing materials both helps and challenges you. The more defined a company's corporate identity, the easier it is for you to focus on fulfilling a certain image. On the other hand, if consumers identify the brand with a fast-paced television commercial with full-motion photography, you might have a harder time translating that style for the Web. At any rate, you must address, and sometimes challenge, the audience's expectations with the visual, structural, and editorial design of the site.

11

LAND ROVER: DON'T CHEAPEN THE MARQUE

Developing a web site for an automobile manufacturer such as Land Rover (http://www.landrover.com/) started with reviewing the brand and studying carefully all the existing corporate communications and marketing material—print collateral, current and past ad campaigns, video, event and competition collateral, owners-only collateral, and vehicle manuals. The print material projected an image of style, sophistication, and elegance (see Figure 1.2).

Figure 1.2

Land Rover's printed marketing materials visually juxtapose the ruggedness of off-road driving with the elegance and sophistication of a luxury automobile.

One program in particular was the Land Rover Invitations, serious off-road driving trips in some of the most beautiful and extreme locations around the world. The trips are guided tours that always involve challenging driving and may also involve skiing, shopping, and other recreational activities. Participants get the opportunity to test the limits of their Land Rover vehicles on the most rugged terrain, yet at the same time experience the luxury of five-star accommodations. We examined all of the brochures for this exclusive and expensive program available for Land Rover owners only (see Figure 1.3).

Figure 1.3
Land Rover's Invitations pieces are especially pronounced examples of how their print materials combine clean serif type and airy, classical page designs with visceral off-road driving imagery.

As part of examining the styles, mood, and message conveyed in the pieces, we drove two hours to the nearest Land Rover dealership to see and experience the cars for ourselves. We could see with our own eyes the craftsmanship of the car. We could see and feel the real walnut and the real leather described in the brochures. By interacting with the product directly, we could make better informed decisions about the design and message of the web site.

We also conducted informal interviews of Land Rover owners to bring us closer to the consumer experience. We asked them what it meant or felt like to own a Land Rover. What they liked best; to find out how they identified with the company's message and the brand. What the intangible qualities attached to owning a Land Rover were. We found a consistent pattern between the interview responses. These were happy car owners, to whom a Land Rover represented freedom, security, confidence, privilege, and craftsmanship.

The Camel Trophy event represented another characteristic in the Land Rover image that takes the elitism, ruggedness, and confidence to the next level. Two drivers from each country have the opportunity to compete in this month-long off-road competition testing endurance and problem-solving skills in such exotic places as Costa Rica, Indonesia, and Borneo. We watched the ESPN news coverage and documentary. We watched people build bridges across streams in the rain forest to transport these convoys of Land Rovers (see Figure 1.4). This event was viewed as representative of the romance, rugged glamour, and excitement of owning a Land Rover.

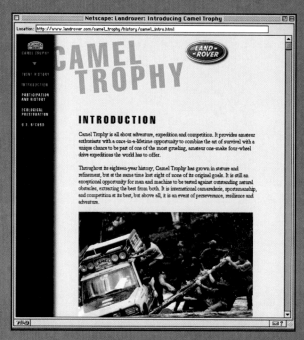

Figure 1.4

Land Rover's involvment in the most grueling of off-road odysseys, the Camel Trophy, best exemplifies several of Land Rover's marque values: individualsim, authenticity, freedom, adventure, guts, and supremacy.

Our research and interviews provided consistent messages associated with the Land Rover image. We had a solid foundation for building a web site. Our first iteration focused on the quality, elegance, and sophistication of owning a Land Rover. We were instructed to follow the motto, "Don't Cheapen the Marque," so we were very cautious.

Land Rover agreed that our work with the site was great. It was Land Rover. The Land Rover people, however, decided that they wanted us to explore more of the confidence, durability, and outdoor lifestyle associated with the brand. They saw the Web as a way to lead their brand strategy. At the time, they had just repositioned the Invitations program and the clothing line was on its way out.

We took advantage of the opportunity to modify the online brand identity at Land Rover's request. The online audience would necessarily be younger than the Land Rover customer who would be attracted to the print ads. We went after the aspects of Land Rover that appealed to us. After all, we were the demographic for which we were designing the site. We planned to create a site for young, hip professionals, a site that would define a brand with integrity, confidence, craftsmanship—a brand whose vehicles were rugged but luxurious, built to withstand, and "the best 4×4 by far."

First, we created a brand board (see Figure 1.5). As discussed in the sidebar, "Creating a Brand Board," later in this chapter, a brand board is "a collage of images, phrases, art, and design that summarizes various aspects of the brand." This included:

◆ Several images of vintage Land Rover shots

◆ An image of a mud-splattered Land Rover logo

◆ Images of the people building the bridge to transport the mud-splattered Land Rovers

◆ Product shots

◆ Photos of remote, exotic-looking places such as the Himalayas or the Red Rocks in Utah

From these images, we could establish a direction for the web site color palette, typography, and layout system (see Figure 1.6). Outdoor colors would undoubtedly be used for the site—earth tones, forest green. A big, bold type was chosen for the headings. We wanted to display meaty, self-reliant, confident type at an angle—something daring, dynamic, and impressive. We also decided to take the big, bold pictures from the brochures and maintain the feeling of space and expansiveness on the web site. No one yet had created full bleeds on a web page, and we didn't want to be limited by the technology at

Figure 1.5

A brand board serves as a visual and emotional touchstone to designers during the conceptualization and design stage of a project. In the case of Land Rover, a brand board would include images such as these.

the time. So, we developed a way to make it happen by placing the image in a table with the width set at 110%. Simple as that. These full bleeds were utilized to create pages with "wow" and charisma. For more details on this technique, please refer to the sidebar, "Making Images Bleed Off the Page," in Chapter 3, "Designing Web Aesthetics."

Today, the site is still fresh and exciting. We made sure we had a clear understanding of Land Rover's brand image and strategy and then were able to run with it.

Figure 1.6

Sitewide, LandRover.com is characterized by its strong typography and bold, uncompromising color palette. Striving for more unified, posteresque page layouts, Adjacency devised a pre-frames way to force images to bleed off the page.

Although having these resources at your disposal provides you with a more specific direction and clues as to how to deliver and strategize your objectives, it is still possible to create a web site without the guidance of other existing corporate communications or marketing pieces, as we have demonstrated in the Rollerblade case study, "Starting from Scratch," found in Chapter 3. Having certain materials readily available is simply an added bonus to your development process, especially if your client considers them to be effective and successful components of their marketing strategies.

The next step, which relates to all projects with or without the availability of existing materials, involves working with your client to determine their future branding strategy in light of their current plans.

DETERMINE CLIENT'S CURRENT AND FUTURE BRANDING STRATEGY

In order to design effectively, you must understand how your client feels about where it stands now and whether or not it wants to modify its consumer brand perception in the future. If the client wants to change, what steps are being taken to achieve this shift? If the client wants to stay on the current path, how does it propose to reinforce the existing brand?

Here are a few questions to ask yourself and your client in order to better understand the strategy:

◆ How does the client want its brand perceived by the public, the industry, and the media?
◆ Who is the client's target demographic?
◆ How does the client view itself vis-à-vis the competition?
◆ How does the client want to differentiate itself?

CREATING A BRAND BOARD

While designing the look and feel, even the functionality and structure, of a web site, you need to keep the character and essence of a brand foremost in your mind. Combined with the documented objectives of the project, the sometimes less-tangible components of the brand will inform nearly every aesthetic and strategic decision you make along the way to finalizing creative work on a site. That said, how can you solidify as much as possible the brand part of the equation?

A useful approach is to create a brand board. In its simplest form, a brand board is a visual prop; a collage of images, phrases, art, and design that summarizes various aspects of a brand:

◆ Style
◆ Consumer types
◆ Associated pop and consumer culture
◆ Packaging and product design
◆ Photography and art
◆ Retail environments
◆ Company history
◆ Signage and advertising
◆ Design inspirations
◆ Corporate culture
◆ Connected personalities and more

This collage can cover an 18×24-inch piece of foam core or an entire wall or fill an entire room. The brand board should be as large as necessary, but as small as possible. A good brand board shows almost everything a designer needs to get a feel for the soul of a brand, the targeted consumer's tastes, lifestyle, and concerns, who the company is and how it wants to be perceived, how the existing brand collateral fits into the project at hand, and what if any refinements or adjustments the project is expected to make to the brand.

A brand board serves as a great starting place for a design team beginning a project. The image selection and cutting and pasting process can contribute to idea generation and design epiphanies yet to come. Often the project's creative director creates a written summary (sometimes with sketches) to get people going in the right direction. Then team members, with this creative brief in hand, collect as many images as they can find that they think embody an aspect of the project, product, and/or brand.

After reconvening, designers post their images and the team discusses them one by one. You need to discuss the vibe or symbolism of the image, how it relates to or reflects the brand, what qualifiers or refinements it may require to fit the brand perfectly, and lastly the image's appropriateness. If enough people, especially the creative director, believe the image fits, it's added to the keepers pile. You do this with every single image. You spend an especially long time discussing the existing collateral and how the web site will relate to it. The process is at once cathartic and reflective. It is a great way to get all of your design team on the same page, or at least within the same chapter.

After you identify and discuss the elements of your brand board, the hard part is over. You need merely bust out the glue sticks and go crazy. Note: Do not use paste. Designers eat paste.

Place your brand board in a place of reverence and refer to it frequently during the design and planning process. Whenever you're agonizing over a decision or simply looking for inspiration, kneel before the brand board and pray.

This step in the design and development process helps pinpoint your client's attitude. By answering these questions, you can better establish your client's competitive advantage over other companies and other sites.

APPRAISING YOUR CLIENT'S COMPETITORS' ONLINE EFFORTS

Speaking of establishing a competitive advantage over other companies and other sites...one of the necessary and effective ways to evaluate your client's brand is to look at your client's competition. No matter what market you're in, you always have competitors. We will help you look beyond the obvious adversaries in your market to understand the scope of your competition. If you want to improve how people interact with your client's web site and products, you must evaluate how competitors are succeeding or failing at using their web sites to promote or support their products. This section discusses how to determine who your competition is and how to anticipate their strategies in order to create a site that surpasses their efforts aesthetically and technically.

REALIZE THAT A WEB SITE IS CONSTANTLY FIGHTING FOR MARKET SHARE

A web site, as with any product, needs to hold up against the products of your competitors. It's not a broadcast medium where people have to see your site or your ad. The web is an interactive medium where the viewer ultimately chooses what he or she wants to see.

Adjacency's goal with every project is to create a site that leads the category online. We understand that if we are creating a site for an automobile manufacturing company, the site will compete with the web sites of automobile magazines, auto clubs, individual enthusiasts, and so on. Identifying that the scope of the competition goes beyond the obvious contenders is necessary because if we design a site that only competes head-on with other automobile manufacturers, we limit the site's potential. The site will most likely be visited only by people when they are considering an automobile purchase.

Figure 1.7

Adjacency created LandRover.com after thoroughly reviewing the top automotive and off-road driving Web sites belonging to publications, events, manufacturers, and so on.

At the same time, we would never stretch the scope so wide that the credibility of the client is reduced. The core business is reinforced by focusing on topics related to and revolving around the client's brand. In the case of Land Rover, we would not include recipes and home improvement tips because Land Rover might then be considered a family car.

DETERMINE WHO THE ONLINE COMPETITION IS

Although there may be more competition than you had expected, you can narrow it down to a manageable few. Let's say you're designing a site for a bicycle manufacturing company. In order to determine who the competitors are, you must pretend you are a consumer interested in bikes in general. Go into an Internet directory such as Yahoo and do a search for "bikes," "bicycling," "biking," and so on. You will see sites for product reviews, manufacturers, and individual bike enthusiasts, just to name a few. From this list, you must pick out the solid contenders.

You are responsible for surfing through these sites and determining how well they have designed the pages, how well they have conveyed information, and how well they have provided compelling and interactive features to engage their audiences. This enables you to see right off the bat who is worthy of being considered competition. If you see a site that provides biking news and articles that is well designed and well-visited based on some sort of robust threaded discussion area, you should add this site to your competition list even though it's not a site for another bicycle manufacturing company. Taking a closer look, you may discover that through this site, users are sharing information with each other about what types of bikes they recommend for certain needs or interests. You need

to be able to identify and harness this need for dialogue and communication on your client's site. A site related in any way to your client's category or product poses a certain amount of competition based on how well they convey information and involve their users.

ROLLERBLADE: APPRAISING THE COMPETITION

Faced with the challenge to create a web site for Rollerblade (http://www.rollerblade.com/), we first studied the product thoroughly. We set out to create the coolest general sport site on the web (see Figure 1.8). Our goal was to make Rollerblade the ambassadors to inline skating so that people would think of Rollerblade when they thought of inline skating; the site needed to define the category. We read all of the inline skating and sporting magazines and conducted focus group interviews for people who skate. Knowing what they did when they weren't skating and what their interests were enabled us to get a comprehensive view of the big picture.

Figure 1.8

Adjacency designed Rollerblade.com, with its big, bold, colorful design, comprehensive product information, lifestyle info, and inline skating resources to define inline skating for the Web.

When we looked at other inline skating manufacturing web sites, we realized that they were not much competition at all. At the basic level, we knew that our solutions for presenting a product catalog would surpass any efforts of Rollerblade's manufacturing competitors. We used huge, bold, in-your-face product shots and used QuickTime VR to present 360-degree views of the skates. Specs about sizes, upgrades, and information on how to change your wheels and bearings were all provided—any information that a customer could possibly want. Every aspect of the site needed to help establish it as *the* online source for reliable and comprehensive inline skating information.

Although the competition provided basic product catalogs and information, they did not address the lifestyle at all. We realized that we would be competing for viewership with any site that is even remotely related to the category, that our biggest competition would be the web sites of inline skating magazines (see Figure 1.9). This meant researching the advertising efforts of snowboarding, skateboarding, and inline skating magazines. We immersed ourselves in the active lifestyle.

Figure 1.9

While researching inline skating-related web sites, most comprehensive sites belonged to skating publications.

We needed more content, information, entertainment, news, lifestyle stories, personality, and character than the magazine sites and all other sites related to inline skating. Our site needed to look cooler, flashier, zingier, and better. By providing general inline skating information, we sought out and managed to attract people who were brand loyalists to Rollerblade's competitors and those who didn't even own inline skates. The goal was to give them cool information that would help them have cooler, happier lives, to make audiences wish they were on the winning team. People's attention needed to be diverted from biking sites—from all other sporting sites, sporting equipment sites, and leisure activity sites.

The web site also had to address the fact that there is no one type of inline skater. This particular consumer audience is quite stratified. Because we wanted to present Rollerblade as the formative resource for all inline skaters, the content would have to satisfy the needs and interests of the following:

◆ **Aggressive skaters:** This subculture, similar to ramp and vertical skateboarders, consists of young, irreverent, predominantly male individualists.

◆ **Inline hockey players:** Predominantly younger males who are into more of the team aspect of the sport.

◆ **Racers:** Speed skaters and marathon long-distance skaters who just want to fly.

◆ **Recreational or fitness enthusiasts:** This group is more of a gender mix of older people found skating leisurely on bike trails and sidewalks.

◆ **Kids:** Eventually they bust out into any one of the other categories, but they lean towards the cool, crazy, and aggressive area.

Therefore, it was apparent that we had to look beyond the obvious competitors to see how they addressed our audience's needs. We learned that the range in our competitors was as complex and varied as the five types of audiences we just identified.

In designing effective web sites, you need not reinvent the wheel. By dissecting your competitors' sites, you can determine their strengths, weaknesses, and failures. You will make aesthetic, and often subjective, judgments in your analysis. If you step back and look at these sites through the eyes of a consumer, you see which features are cool and which are lame. Don't use the lame stuff. Improve on the cool stuff. With this information, you can build a strong site that eclipses the competition.

DEVELOPING YOUR CLIENT'S ONLINE CORPORATE COMMUNICATIONS STRATEGY

Because you are the web expert to whom your client has turned for help in developing their web site, you need to be able to guide them through the process of developing a new part of their corporate communications and marketing strategies on the web. To some degree, you might need to educate them in terms of understanding the web medium—its advantages and capabilities as well as its limitations. You need to sit down with your client and discuss how you might reinvent the brand in the context of the web. In doing so, you must also identify the aspects of the brand best suited for the web medium.

REINVENT THE BRAND IN THE CONTEXT OF THE WEB

Every company represents and communicates certain things to the media and the industry. Different components of these ideas appeal to people using the web. You must understand that you are addressing a certain strata of the consumer based on the online audience.

Land Rover's existing print ads, for example, had a very elegant, sophisticated look. Its targeted online audience was a younger, more rugged, outdoor type that did not fit this classic style. Because the company knew and understood its users well, it left the beautiful calligraphic, initial-caps-look for print and went for something totally new for the web (see Figure 1.10).

Help your client see and understand that the web is a golden opportunity to reach different parts of their consumer base and achieve different goals that might otherwise not be possible. Interactivity on the web serves as the most obvious advantage of creating a web site to support a client's corporate communications strategy. In Chapter 4, we discuss the meaning of interactivity and how to build interactive features into your web site. For now, keep in mind that the web offers your client a means to develop a fresh component to their corporate image—one that can be easily updated and expanded.

DETERMINE WHAT ABOUT THE BRAND CAN BEST BE CONVEYED THROUGH THE WEB

Web site features that take advantage of the web's interconnectivity best reinforce the brand. The web site represents an opportunity for a company to prove that there's something behind all of the hype, that the company is for real, and that it means business.

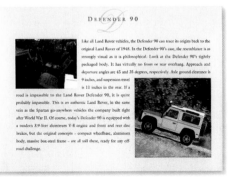

Figure 1.10

Land Rover allowed Adjacency to design LandRover.com to depart somewhat from the company's traditional print aesthetic to explore the more rugged, adventure-seeking aspects of the brand.

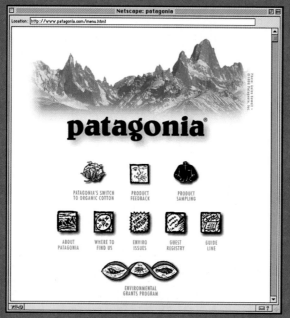

Figure 1.11

Patagonia's web site is the furthest thing from a staid corporate image piece. Four of the nine main site sections are dedicated to environmental education and activism and backcountry sports resources.

For the Patagonia web site, we determined a need to position the company online in a way that differentiated it from other clothing manufacturers. Creating an online catalog wasn't an option because other clothing companies already do that. We needed to pick out the brand features that would best be conveyed through the web. Patagonia's credibility online as an innovative company that went online because it had a reason to, not because it was a fad, needed to be established. We had to help Patagonia make the transition into the communications era without alienating its customers, many of whom were already distrustful of the Internet and technology in general.

Indeed, we had quite an endeavor ahead of us. All of these considerations needed to be taken into account so that the web site added another dimension to the company's image. We had to be very careful. If we did it wrong, we would confuse the image and portray the company inaccurately.

To achieve our objectives, we decided to show how Patagonia stands for more than just clothing sales. The web site was used to illustrate the humanitarian and environmental aspects of the company. We discussed how the company uses organic materials and how nonorganic crop harvesting damages the environment because of all the chemicals and pesticides used. Information was provided on how Patagonia donates a percentage of its profits to certain environmental protection organizations. We wanted to show how Patagonia is a company with a conscience while empowering and enlightening visitors with information (see Figure 1.12).

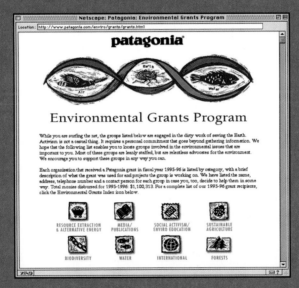

Figure 1.12

Patagonia uses their web site to publicize the various environmental groups they support. To quote Patagonia, "While you are surfing the Net, (these groups) are engaged in the dirty work of saving the Earth."

At the same time, we made sure that the depictions of the clothing and merchandise were consistent with a serious clothing company dedicated to service and quality. We emphasized how the clothes were comfortable, functional pieces to be worn and used in the extreme conditions such as the wilderness. The clothes are equipment, not fashion statements.

All of these objectives helped shape Patagonia's strategy for the web site, where we hoped to create a unique and effective tool for the company to communicate with its customers.

When Specialized, a company historically perceived as a hard-core bike company with the best high-end bikes, migrated the technology downward to reach everyday consumers, it needed to readjust how it represented itself. How did Adjacency achieve this through the web site? By emphasizing the company's commitment to the bicycling sport. We created a forum on the site for people to exchange information about their favorite bike trails. It began with a listing of Specialized's favorite spots and expanded to enable consumers to communicate with the company and with each other (see Figure 1.13).

If you can create a place that you know you would appreciate as a consumer, you're going to reinforce the brand.

SUMMARY

As we have discussed in this chapter, there is definitely more to creating a web site than throwing a bunch of text and graphics together on separate pages. Before you choose each word, each link, each typeface, each graphic, and each color, you must first have a clear understanding of what message and identity these elements convey together as a whole. In other words, you must have a solid understanding of your client's brand and all of the values, issues, and implications attached to it. This understanding serves as the foundation for building your site. The foundation grows stronger the more information you have about the company, the market, and the competition. With these internal and external factors in mind at all times, you can make more-informed decisions for a stronger, clearer design and structure of the web site.

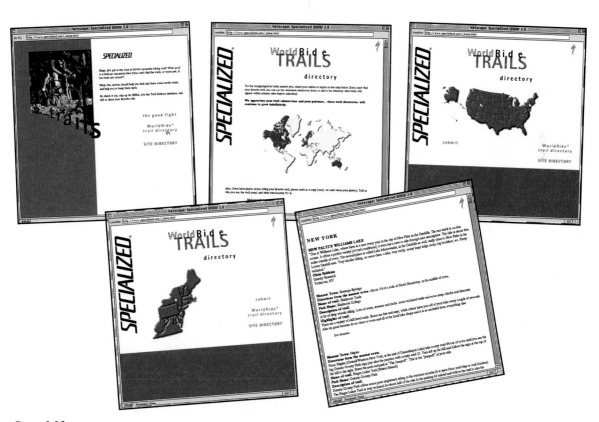

Figure 1.13

Specialized's World Ride Web directories provide site visitors with the locations of great mountain biking trails and road rides. Adjacency conceptualized such features to position Specialized.com as the muscle, brain, and soul of biking on the web.

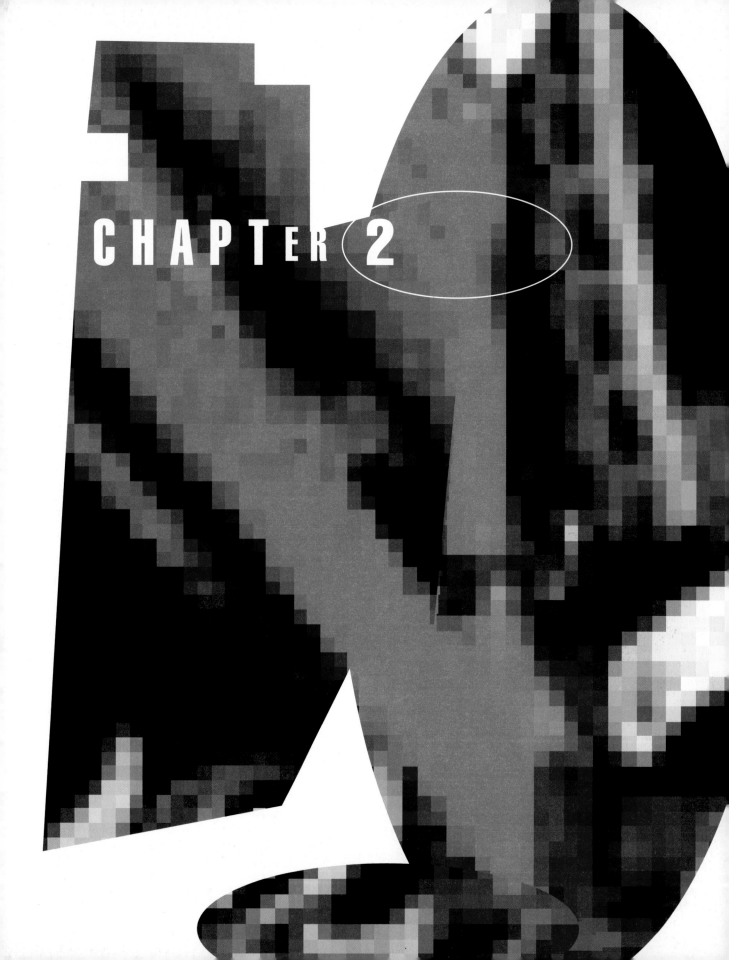

CHAPTER 2

NOW THAT YOU HAVE A GRASP FOR YOUR CLIENT'S CORPORATE IDENTITY AND PHILOSOPHIES,

YOU ARE READY TO DIVE INTO THE NITTY-GRITTY OF CREATING A WEB SITE. DON'T BE SUR-

PRISED, BUT WE MUST WARN YOU TO RESIST THE TEMPTATION OF DIVING DIRECTLY INTO

PRODUCTION—CREATING GRAPHICS DEVELOPING **SITE**

AND WRITING COPY. THE NITTY-GRITTY **STRATEGY** AND

BEGINS WITH PLANNING THE SITE STRATEGY AND **STRUC**TURE

ARCHITECTURE. AS WITH ANY "CONSTRUCTION" PROJECT, WHETHER IT IS BUILDING

A SKYSCRAPER, WRITING A BOOK, OR KNITTING A SWEATER, YOU NEED A SOLID BLUE-

PRINT OR PLAN IN ORDER TO START BUILDING OR CREATING. WITHOUT SPECIFIC

STRATEGIES TO ACCOMPLISH THE GIVEN OBJECTIVES, YOU EXPEND VALUABLE

RESOURCES AND MATERIALS ON A SITE THAT MISSES THE TARGET.

THIS CHAPTER HELPS YOU DETERMINE THE WHO, WHAT, HOW, AND WHY OF YOUR WEB

SITE. WE GUIDE YOU THROUGH SETTING OBJECTIVES, ISOLATING TARGET AUDIENCES

AND THEIR NEEDS, AS WELL AS ORGANIZING YOUR WEB SITE ARCHITECTURE.

OBJECTIVES OR GOALS REINFORCE THE PURPOSE OF THE SITE, PROVIDING CLEAR PATHS

TO A SPECIFIC DIRECTION. WITHOUT THIS FOCUS, YOUR MESSAGE BECOMES DILUTED AND

WEAK. IDENTIFYING AND UNDERSTANDING YOUR AUDIENCE ENABLES YOU TO CREATE A MORE

EFFECTIVE WEB SITE. DESIGNING A WEB SITE FOR THE WRONG KIND OF AUDIENCE MAKES AS much sense as knitting a children's size sweater for a grown man. Similarly, creating a web site designed as "one size fits all" may not be as strong or as compelling as a site that "fits" a particular audience. Finally, we discuss how to organize your content and plan the underlying structure for your site. You need a definite blueprint for the different directories and content areas in your web site in order to gauge your artistic and technical needs.

DEFINING SITE OBJECTIVES

The key to developing effective site strategies and structures is defining solid site objectives. Most corporate web sites endeavor to convey information about that company's products and services and encourage customers to act on information they receive. Each web site has its own set of objectives, but here is a list of basic objectives common to corporate web sites. They may help and inspire you in your own web site development:

◆ **Establish the company as an expert in its category.** As discussed elsewhere in this book, when you create a web site around a particular topic or within a specific industry, you are competing for usership with nearly every other related site on the web. The primary reason for this is that you must provide ancillary information in most instances to lure visitors to your site. Therefore, nine times out of ten the person or organization with the best, most compelling, or most usable information wins. Your content must be accurate and useful, and it must establish you as one of the visible experts within that

area. Comprehensive, valuable information breeds credibility; credibility breeds trust, and consumer trust is one of the most valuable currencies to a brand.

◆ **Provide comprehensive product and service information.** Many consumers visit corporate web sites expressly for product information. The majority of Adjacency's most popular client sites see almost half of their total site activity occurring within their product sections. What's more the web is an excellent medium in which to organize and present large amounts of detailed information. Companies can direct consumers to their web site for searchable product databases and animated product use tutorials. A general rule is for a company to strive to reproduce all sales and support literature and information on their web site so it serves as a comprehensive, constantly updated corporate library for consumers, dealers and resellers, the media, and partners.

◆ **Differentiate itself from its competitors.** A key to Adjacency's success in building corporate web sites that stand out is that we take differentiation from competitors' web sites very seriously. Your site needs to be better, more noteworthy, more useful, and more memorable than the competition.

◆ **Convey key branding messages.** A web site needs to be integrated into a company's overall corporate communications program. It must be in synch with, amplify, and elaborate on key advertising messages promoted in other mediums. A web site written and designed in a vacuum can do much more damage than staying off the web altogether.

◆ **Learn more about the site's users: conduct demographic and psychographic research.** The direct marketing and market research component of the web is quickly becoming its most compelling characteristic. What do you want to know about consumers? Ask them. If you can give them proper incentive to do so, they may very well provide you with all the information you request...and more.

◆ **Generate sales leads.** The web is a beautiful medium in that you can sow and reap using the same tool. You may have the luxury of gathering potential customer info that you can respond to yourself, though dealer referrals are equally useful.

◆ **Foster positive investor relations.** Early on the web became very popular with investors. The web continues to be an ideal environment for investors to retrieve and send information because of its global coverage, updatability, and inherent timeliness. Online investor relations has become more of an expectation than a perk.

◆ **Provide resources to the news media.** Any reporter working on a deadline can appreciate the value of a medium that is entirely searchable and accessible 24 hours per day, seven days a week, and that enables two-way instantaneous communication. Examine how you're providing trade news and general news media organizations with information about your company. Odds are if it's offline, it's slower and costlier than email and the web.

◆ **Engage in effective online recruiting.** One of the earliest and most diehard web usergroups was academia. It remains one of the best research and job finding tools for students. Want qualified employment leads? Post your job openings and solicit email applications online where people all over the world interested in your particular industry can, with the help of an Internet directory and links from industry organization sites, find you.

◆ **Encourage repeat return traffic.** An initial visit to your site is a small victory in a game where repeated, prolonged exposure to web sites and their messages separate the good sites from the great ones. Ultimately, the quality of the design, freshness and profundity of the content, and meaningfulness of the functionality of a site determine the amount of repeat traffic it can command. The effectiveness of such components can be appreciably enhanced through smart and repeated promotion of your site online and off.

◆ **Preempt and eclipse competitors' online efforts.** As more web sites launch daily, second place within a category is becoming less and less noteworthy. If you can't afford to do more with your site than your competitors, do things better.

◆ **Increase awareness of company news and recent promotions and developments.** Your web site is probably the cheapest and most quickly updatable weapon in your PR arsenal. There is no printing or mailing to worry yourself with. The best sites are updated frequently and with as little effort as possible.

- **Complement and mirror other corporate communications.** In short, a web site should be an integral part of a company's corporate communications strategy. If used properly, a web site, with its detailed, diverse, and updated content can serve up the final blow in a sales and branding process initiated hours, days, perhaps weeks before, well apart from the Internet in a broadcast or paper-based advertising venue.

DETERMINING TARGET AUDIENCE(S) AND THEIR NEEDS

Design involves more than the end product. You cannot determine whether or not something is well designed without seeing a user interact with it. Therefore, you can't design an effective web site without knowing your audience. This task involves determining who is currently going to the site (if you are redesigning it), who you want to visit the site in the future, and what reasons users have in visiting this site.

WHO WILL BE USING THE SITE?

Just as you may already have existing corporate communications and marketing materials to work with in developing a web site, you may, in fact, already have an actual web site with which to start if you are brought in to redesign the entire site or add a new section. In this case, you should ask your client the following questions about their existing web audience. If your client has established their target audience, you need to be able to see a mental picture of who this person is and find ways to make the web site that person's web site. That person needs to feel as if the site was created with his or her specific needs or interests in mind. He or she must regard the content in the site as relevant and important information. You can help your client determine whether or not the target audience is appropriate by reviewing the following questions for a project where a target audience has not yet been established.

In these instances where you need to build a web site from concept to completion, you need to step back and understand who makes up the general web viewing population in order to determine who might comprise the target audience (or audiences, as the case may be).

Here are a few questions to help you understand who your audience is and who your potential audiences might be:

- Who is the average Internet user? Gender? Age? Education? Hobbies and interests? Level of computer savviness?
- What people within that group are going to be attracted to your product, your brand? In other words, who online would be interested?
- What are your client's consumer demographics and psychographics? Gender? Age? Education? Hobbies and interests? Are they techno-savvy?
- Can you sample a consumer group to see if the people you are trying to reach have any recognizable online habits? Do they spend a lot of time on one page, or do they jump quickly from page to page within a site? Do they jump quickly from site to site? Do they rely on the web as a primary source of news or purchasing information? Do they shop online?

Obviously, the means of coming by this information are not always readily available. Often these kinds of questions can be asked only after the first generation of the site has been developed. Once you have a site online and are receiving regular visitors, you can solicit feedback from your users and see what they would most like to see available on the site. Ask them what they were looking for when they came to the site. Did they find it? Was it hard to find? These sorts of questions can help guide additional site development and targeting. In entering the first redesign of the PowerBar site, for example, we solicited information from the site visitors who had registered as PowerUsers, asking them to fill out a brief redesign survey that helped determine what improvements to the site would benefit them most.

Although it is rare, you may occasionally have opportunity to observe a large sample of your target audience actually using and interacting with a site in person. Adjacency, for example, sent two representatives to Interbike, a national trade show for the cycling industry, to demonstrate the Specialized web site to bike dealers and enthusiasts attending the show. By observing their reactions to the site, we were able to make navigational improvements that made it easier to move through the site.

Use the sidebar, "Developing a User Profile," in this section as a reference checklist and guide for defining your target audience. Refer back to it throughout your web site's development process to make sure that you stay on target.

DEVELOPING A USER PROFILE

Great web sites beget great communication, and great communication demands that you understand the needs and wants of those with whom you are communicating. Furthermore, you must understand how the individual is accepting and using the information. A user profile begins to lay the foundation for this understanding.

Many companies have existing brand and consumer profiles for their products or services. No need to re-create the wheel here. Work with your client and their strategic marketing partners to access existing market research. Read it. Comprehend it. Then read it again. It is invaluable information.

Keep in mind that you may have multiple audiences for the site. Some users may be consumers of your client's products, while others may be members of the press, and others may be prospective employees. Each potential audience needs a profile. This might require you to access people and information from a wide array of corporate departments, including marketing, sales, human resource development, public relations, and investor relations.

As the use of the web matures, more departments and individuals from corporations are becoming involved in the process of web site creation. This undoubtedly means more committees and more meetings. The properly prepared user profile can help deflect potential conflicts by providing early consensus on the who, what, how, when, and where questions regarding the user.

To create a user profile, try to determine the following characteristics about your target audience(s):

Demographics

- Age
- Gender
- Education level
- Geographic areas
- Household income
- Media consumption habits
- Ethnicity and/or nationality
- web usage level

Characteristics—Needs/Wants

- What information do they desire?
- How are they going to use the information?
- How often might they access this information?
- Where will they be accessing the information from?
- How might these needs change over time?
- What level of web knowledge do they possess?

- What other web sites do they access? Why?
- How do they use the web in general?
- In what ways do they use your client's products and services?
- Why do they use the product or service?
- How do they purchase the product or service?
- Where do they purchase the product?
- How do they find out about the product or service?
- Are they buying on price, service, quality, other?

Like any good marketer, your objective is to get inside the head of the user and understand them. You are developing a communication format that will be the basis for an ongoing dialog between your client and their clients for years to come. As such, it must maintain your client's corporate identity and voice while being immediately approachable and easily comprehensible by the target audiences. The properly prepared profile becomes the touchstone for this entire process.

Moving beyond personality traits, habits, and interests, the next step to understanding your target audience involves determining what kind of equipment they might have to view your web site. Does your typical user view your site on Netscape Navigator or Microsoft Internet Explorer? What version do they have? These details determine what enhanced features you can include or should exclude from your site. Are your visitors on a Macintosh or a Windows machine? The difference in how text is displayed and how elements align is dramatic. How big or small is your user's monitor? If you create a background tile, does someone with a big monitor see the tile repeat beyond where you

intended it to be seen? If you create a long, scrolling page, to what extent is someone on a 640×480 monitor affected negatively by the experience of using this page? Is your target audience capable of seeing 256 colors onscreen? Or millions? This section's sidebar, "Accommodating the Multitude of Browsers and Platforms," thoroughly details the cross-browser and cross-platform issues you must consider in developing a web site as well as possible solutions. The next chapter, "Designing Web Aesthetics," discusses the various ways to handle these issues, as well as issues involving monitor sizes and color depth.

ACCOMMODATING THE MULTITUDE OF BROWSERS AND PLATFORMS

Clients want the best from their web site. They want it to conform to their existing corporate identity, to follow from their existing print collateral. Building web sites that strive to rival print media in complexity and design has become a new art. This is what David Siegel calls the art of third-generation site design.

Although you may love building sites that push the limits of HTML, use pixel-level positioning, simulate full-page bleeds, and use complex table-based layouts, these techniques can often fall apart when rendered on a platform or browser other than the one used for development. Accommodating all the possible end-user scenarios is a daunting prospect. Upon realizing that different browsers do different things with HTML, many developers throw up their hands and resign themselves to building sites that don't quite do what they could.

Fortunately, there are ways of overcoming this problem.

The easiest means is to have a user choose a site that is designed for his or her browser. Obviously it isn't feasible to build a different version of a site for every available browser, so at Adjacency we try to filter users into two broad categories: those who are using the latest version of Netscape Navigator or Internet Explorer, and those who are not.

Based on this strategy, we ask users to choose between an "enhanced" site and a "lite" site. The enhanced site takes advantage of features available only in the newest crop of browsers, such as JavaScript, Java, plug-in content, and frames. The lite site is built to enable people with older browsers or slower connections to access the same content, without all the bells and whistles.

This clears the first hurdle, but the browser balancing act doesn't end there. Even the newest browsers can still do quite different things with your code. One of the most notable differences is in browser offset. Browser offset is the amount, in screen pixels, that the browser indents from the top left corner of the window before rendering the page (see Figure 2.1). This difference comes into play when you are trying to place transparent GIFs in specific places on a background image.

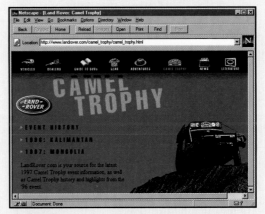

Figure 2.1

An example of how differing browser offsets can affect page layout. Notice how the Land Rover logo and the "Site Menu" head don't quite line up with the background image.

Fortunately, we have found that these differences fall largely along the lines of platform. That is, the Macintosh version of Netscape behaves slightly differently from the Windows version. Similarly, the Macintosh version of Explorer behaves differently from the Windows version. But the Mac version of Netscape renders code remarkably like the Mac version of Explorer, and the same is true on the Windows platform.

The next step, then, is to determine what kind of computer people are using. When users click the "enhanced site" link, their request is passed through a CGI script that parses their platform information out of the HTTP request. Windows and X-Windows users are redirected to a Windows site, while Mac users are served their own version. This CGI, which we call plat.pl, is a custom Perl script. For more information on using this script on your web site, please visit the companion site for this book at `http://www.adj.com/killer/`.

It may sound like a lot of work building a separate site for two platforms (as well as a lite site), but in fact it only *appears* as if we have two versions of the site. In actuality, the only thing different about the two versions of the site is the background image used. To create the illusion of separate Mac and Windows sites, we take advantage of a feature in the Unix file system called symbolic links. A symbolic link is simply a placeholder file that points to another file. So all the pages and foreground elements in the Windows version of the site are actually symbolic links to their counterparts in the Mac version.

The creation of these symbolic links is automated using a script called makesyms. This script scans an entire web site, creating a win directory with symbolic links to all of the files in the site. If it sees a folder called win_bk, it creates a symbolic link to the background image in that folder instead of using the original. By shifting this background to account for browser offset, we can achieve faithful reproduction across platforms (see Figure 2.2).

Figure 2.2
Creating a win directory enables us to account for the browser offset on different platforms.

More information on using this script also is available on the companion book site.

Elegant as it was when it was first developed, this solution is starting to show its age. Other differences in browsers have arisen, forcing us and other developers to start looking for alternative solutions.

One alternative is to use JavaScript. JavaScript has built-in objects that tell you about the browser and the platform being used. If, for example, you're using Netscape 3 on a Power Mac, JavaScript could be inserted in the page you're viewing that would tell whomever created the site that `navigator.appVersion = 3.01 (Macintosh; I; PPC)`. The site creator could then use this information to redirect you to certain content. Again, this method involves some duplication of effort and is limited by the fact that it works only on Netscape Navigator 2 and higher and Internet Explorer 3 and higher.

A third alternative is to build the site using frames. Frames are often scorned but are a blessing in that they enable you to set the margin width and margin height in a way that is consistent across all major new browsers and platforms. (Internet Explorer had a similar attribute added to the <BODY> tag, but it doesn't work in Netscape. If it's not one, it's the other...) An excellent example of this technique can be found on the Lufthansa USA site at http://www.lufthansa-usa.com/. The initial page of this site is just one big frame with the MARGINWIDTH and MARGINHEIGHT set to 1, with the document menu.html loaded into that frame:

```
<FRAMESET ROWS="100%,*" BORDER=0 FRAME-
BORDER=NO BORDERCOLOR="000000">

<FRAME  SRC="menu.html"  NAME="mainpage"
SCROLLING="auto"  MARGINHEIGHT=1  MARGIN-
WIDTH=1 RESIZE=NO>

</FRAMESET>
```

(Actually, the minimum value for MARGINWIDTH and MARGINHEIGHT is 0, but Netscape doesn't recognize values less than 1.) This technique enables us to have complete control over element positioning using tables and be certain that things look the same across the browser-platform divide because it eliminates the offset problem.

The frame method has the additional benefit of enabling us to separate older browsers from newer ones, as older browsers typically don't support frames. We can then use the NOFRAMES tag to take those users without frames directly to the lite site without having to ask.

As if that weren't enough, there is yet another alternative on the horizon, and its name is Cascading Style Sheets, or CSS. If you haven't heard of CSS, you will. Especially if you turn to the section on it in Chapter 3, where we explore CSS in greater depth.

After you pinpoint the obvious interested parties in your site, you might also want to attract people who don't necessarily know that they need or want your product. People interested in the general category of your brand will be drawn to your site as a solution to their needs. The more you attract non-brand-specific audiences, the more you reinforce the credibility and staying power of your product. Seldom do repeat visitors investigate a site out of mere curiosity of a specific brand. One visit tends to satisfy the curiosity. Beyond that, people need specific reasons to revisit a site. Users and consumers need solutions they can apply to their daily lives. If a site can provide useful applications, meaningful information, and engaging dialog between the users and the company, then it can inspire people to visit again and again.

WHAT WILL VISITORS BE COMING FOR?

After determining your audience(s), you must determine what they want. You must understand the users' needs in order to organize and package your product information in such a way that they can use and appreciate it.

Here is a list of the things that people usually look for when they reach a web site:

◆ **Information**: People want information about the products and services offered and where and how to buy them. They want to know who the company is, how they can trust the company, and maybe even how to get a job with the company.

◆ **News**: You probably want to keep visitors abreast of relevant recent developments such as product announcements, investor news, trade show and events updates, favorable product reviews or news coverage, industry news, new personnel appointments, partnership deals, co-promotions and more. Many people look to companies' web sites for the latest, most reliable information regarding that company, their products, and the industry.

◆ **Interaction**: People like the option of contacting a company through their web site to ask questions, request literature, or offer their opinions. Many visitors appreciate being given an online venue to interact with fellow visitors.

◆ **Entertainment**: People want to have fun and enjoy getting the information they need. Though recently whipped to death, the concept of infotainment is a valid one. The more you can integrate corporate information and messages into more general or diversionary content, the greater the number of people that consume it.

◆ **Freebies**: Free products or prizes, or the chance of winning free products or prizes, is often the sort of incentive many site visitors need to spur them to visit the site and/or complete survey forms or sign-up for emailing and direct mailing lists.

When trying to determine what your audience wants and expects from your client, why not just ask them? You can gather valuable feedback by means of a focus group, which can be as simple as coming up with a questionnaire for your acquaintances to fill out or as involved as bringing in a group of consumers to give feedback on designs of a new product.

It helps to interview or survey consumers and ask them what they want to see from a web site. You must try to determine what they might use the site for or expect to find. It's always a good idea to run feature ideas by them and see what they think. Similarly, you can test initial creations to see if the consumer thinks they fit the brand or stir interest.

When your site is nearly finished, you may want to conduct a usability test in which you sit people down at workstations running the site and observe the way they interact with it. In addition, have them complete a survey or review of the site navigation and interface. Many companies have made interface refinements shortly before site launch in response to results from such tests.

Perhaps the most valuable form of user feedback is the online survey. One of the primary uses of site redesigns and phased site expansions or updates is to address user complaints, suggestions, and praise. Don't be afraid to give site visitors an incentive to tell you what they think of your work. Ask them how they feel about the site design, certain content areas, site updating, user interface and navigation, and more. Find out what you're doing wrong and fix it, what people appreciate and amplify it, and implement strategies that work site-wide. People love offering opinions and suggestions, especially if they realize just how much you appreciate their input and that you make changes based on their input.

Adjacency used focus group testing when redesigning the site we created for PowerBar. After working with the client to generate a list of questions, we built an online survey form for the site's most frequent visitors, the PowerUsers. In it, we had them rate the site in terms of content, navigation, design, personality, speed, and overall feel, as well as what they found most appealing, least desirable, what sports they wanted to see added, what other information they wanted to see added, and what their three favorite web sites were. We demonstrated to them that we wanted to serve them better. What's more, we showed that their opinions were respected.

POWERBAR: DEVELOPING SITE OBJECTIVES AND STRATEGY

How do you make a web site about an energy bar? PowerFood approached us with the need to get PowerBar into more customer hands. Based on a preliminary survey conducted among a core group of PowerBar users, PowerFood determined that their users were definitely online. In addition, they wanted to tap into the growth of the web to make sure that they were on top of new marketing opportunities. PowerFood has always been a company that tries to market in unique ways. When they came to us, they were ready to explore what the web had to offer, as well as consolidate all of the PowerBar marketing collateral—TV, events, and print—into one cohesive message on a web site.

When we started the development of the site for PowerFood, we decided to focus on the benefits of using its PowerBar products (`http://www.powerbar.com/`) (see Figure 2.3). We realized that the best way to do this was to appeal to PowerFood customers by addressing their active lifestyles and issues concerning health, fitness, and nutrition—to communicate more than the product.

Figure 2.3

Though Adjacency realized PowerBar.com shouldn't stray far from the reason for the site—the products—we sought to create a site that would leverage PowerFood's greatest strength: PowerBar products appeal to a diverse group of ultra-loyal consumers across a wide range of sports and ability levels.

Therefore the best way to approach this site was to think about who would be using PowerFood products. What kind of person eats PowerBars? The average PowerBar user is involved heavily in a variety of sports, exercises frequently, and cares about nutrition. We had to build a web site that would appeal to this type of person. Based on this knowledge, we figured that we would have to address different issues and communicate specific kinds of information for this person to find the site useful enough to use it over and over again.

First, we needed to provide information about the PowerBar products. On the site, we included as much detailed nutritional information as possible. Although we didn't want the product to be the only focus and reason for the site, the PowerBar product serves as the fulcrum upon which the other areas are balanced (see Figure 2.4).

Figure 2.4
Though the site is fundamentally about PowerBar products, PowerBar.com would not be as popular as it is were it not for the lifestyle information and sports resources. The challenge was to build and maintain a viable online community around energy products.

Second, we needed to provide company history about PowerFood and why it is an authority on its products. We knew that users would need some kind of background information to be able to trust the company and therefore the product (see Figure 2.5).

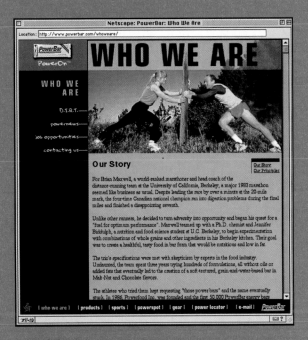

Figure 2.5
Company and product history is a valuable compo-nent of any brand's value. PowerBar.com tells the story of a world-class marathoner who learned first-hand of the need for a more nutritionally solid athlet-ic source.

Third, because we knew that product information alone would not drive return traffic, we needed to build a sense of community among PowerBar users. A forum was needed for these people to be able to communicate with each other and with the PowerFood company. Another PowerBar case study with the specifics of building an online community is in Chapter 4, "Designing and Building Interactivity."

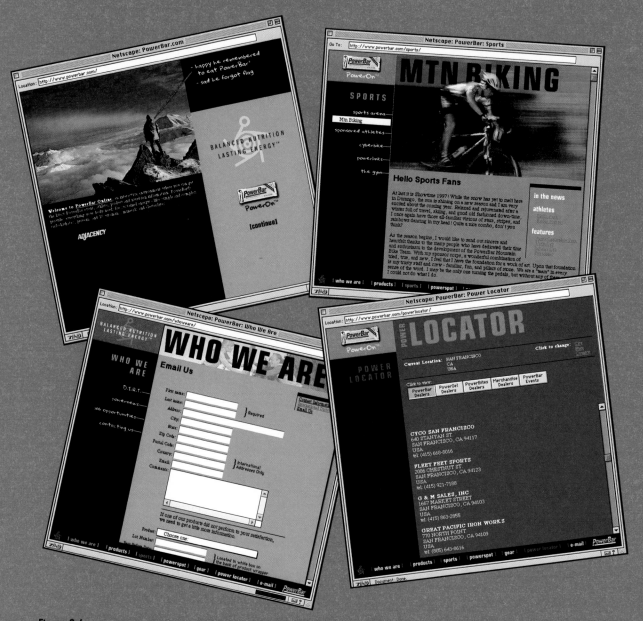

Figure 2.6

Two of PowerBar.com's major objectives is to creat consistent return traffic and visitor interaction and contribution. The site's PowerSpot section is the social hub of the web site.

Based on these general aspects, we developed a set of objectives for the site in conjunction with PowerFood in order to have clearly defined goals and a direction for the site. All of the following points fall under an overarching goal for the site to "develop a cool and engaging online community where athletic and healthy individuals attuned to the needs of their bodies will gather with frequency," according to Tim Tumbleson, PowerFood's interactive marketing manager.

1. Inform people about the products.

2. Create a fresh and constantly updated site that would drive return traffic.

3. Accommodate equally all PowerBar users no matter which sports or sports communities they are involved in.

4. Get as much demograhic information as possible and create dialog with consumers.

5. Always discuss the product in the context of the users.

6. Create and foster an online community among PowerBar users— everyone from complete recreational enthusiasts to the pro-sponsored athletes.

When these objectives were established, we determined the strategies for accomplishing them. Just as it is important to define goals and objectives to achieve a specific direction for the site, it is crucial to set up strategies for executing and following through with them.

In order to create an informative web site, we provided meticulous information and descriptions about each product; more information than you could possibly want! We wanted to demonstrate in numbers and figures how nutritional and how thoroughly researched and scientifically tested the products are.

To create a timely site that would drive return traffic, we created a PowerUser system that customizes the site according to your interests (see Figure 2.7). Whenever you log in as a PowerUser, you get only the information pertaining to you. You see the latest news and happenings about sporting events in your area—and only about the sports that you like. Up-to-date event coverage is provided for a variety of sports on the site. Each year, PowerFood sponsors over 4,000 participatory sporting events. We also host content from sponsored athletes who contribute columns and pictures to the site on a regular basis.

Figure 2.7

The PowerUser feature serves in many ways as a preview of things to come web-wide. PowerUsers are delivered customized versions of the site based on their specific interests, frequency of visits, and geographic location.

To accommodate PowerBar users interested in a variety of sports and to attract people from diverse sporting cultures, we made sure that every sport got its own section within the site. The PowerUser system simplifies the site for people so that you have the opportunity to create your own custom site menu for the sports you are interested in, but you will always have the opportunity to view the other sections. You are never locked out of any section.

In order to get as much demographic information as possible and create direct dialogs with consumers, we have PowerUsers fill out a questionnaire before they enter the PowerUser area (see Figure 2.8). There are 6,000 registered users who see the survey and have the opportunity to give feedback on how to improve the site as well as provide information about what their favorite flavors are.

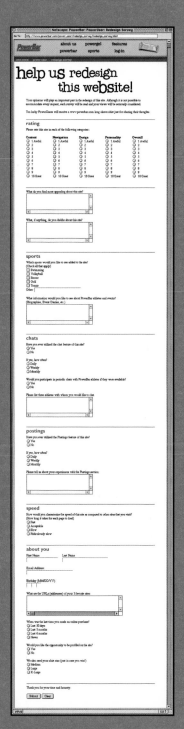

Figure 2.8

Using the PowerBar.com site redesign questionnaire, Adjacency solicited feedback from PowerUsers, the most frequent visitors to the site. The resulting information assisted us during the redesign of the site.

In order to foster an online community among PowerBar users, we created the "Power Spot" area for visitors to submit stories, photographs, favorite places to exercise, and sport club listings, as well as participate in chats and threaded discussions.

 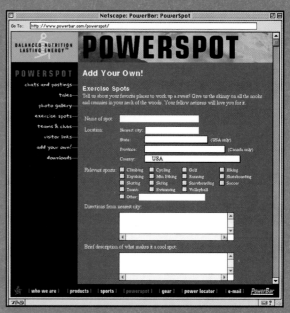

Figure 2.9

Visitors to PowerBar.com are encouraged to participate by using the PowerSpot to contribute their favorite sports locations, photos of their athletic exploits, stories, links to their favorite sports-related web sites, and team and club listings, and to participate in live chats and threaded discussion groups.

Clearly, the process for determining web site objectives and strategies is an involved, ambitious task! Remember that both parts of the exercise are necessary. You need to set goals as well as plan how to execute and follow through with the goals. Before this step, you must clearly understand the company and brand you're dealing with. You can also simplify every step of the process by communicating constantly and clearly with your client.

Whenever possible, you should leverage off existing user information that your client may already have. Kemper Funds, for example, deals directly with its customers. Based on a customer survey conducted by the company, Kemper Funds knows what percentage uses computers, uses the Internet, what they use the Internet for, whether or not they use online banking, and so on. Your client is a valuable resource.

DESIGNING WEB SITE ARCHITECTURE

This section guides you through the process of mapping out your web site structure in order to create effective information designs and prototypes. Here we recommend standard procedures for receiving and cataloging site materials, help you organize and group your content areas, and discuss how to direct visitor flow through cross-navigability. All of these elements in designing the web site architecture contribute to a more manageable site for you and your client as well as result in a more usable and intuitive site for your users. The more organized and carefully considered your plans are, the easier it is to maintain and grow.

DESIGN A MANAGEABLE AND EASILY UPDATABLE SITE

At the beginning of a project, you should clearly communicate the design process to your client. You should define the specific roles and expectations to avoid any confusion. The following suggestions for creating a standardized process can make your life simpler and easier.

◆ Work through one primary contact person from the client company and make sure that the client is dealing with primarily one

person on your end. Certainly, more than two people are involved in the development of the web site! Having specific point people to oversee the clients' needs as well as the different action items of the production on your end minimizes or hopefully eliminates any confusion in the process.

◆ Clearly explain the content formats you require so that the client knows exactly what you need. If you need graphics, let them know if you need an EPS, a PICT, a TIFF, or an original Photoshop file. If you need copy from your client, let them know if you prefer a Microsoft Word document, an email, or a SimpleText file. Be clear about whether or not you expect printouts of any digital files.

◆ Set up a system for checking and receiving materials so that you can easily chart the project's progress as well as have a record for yourself. Some people may find it convenient to receive the materials as they are ready through perhaps email or an FTP site. (See the sidebar in this chapter regarding FTP site setup and protocol.) Other people may find it more manageable to receive everything all at once, or at least in large chunks on some sort of disk format. In one case, Adjacency purchased a Zip drive for a client to simplify the delivery process. Whatever delivery methods or procedures you have should be clearly communicated and explained to your clients.

FTP SITE SETUP AND ETIQUETTE

In working with any client, your client contact sends new content on a regular basis, especially during the initial phase of site development. Many people assume that the best way to transfer such files is to email them as attachments, but in most cases, this is a poor solution that goes against many long-established Internet conventions.

Quite often, the files your client sends can range anywhere from 100K to 100 MB. Email was designed for sending simple text messages, which are usually under 32K in size. In order to be transferred across the Net using email, a file must be encoded as text (which makes it even larger), broken into smaller packets, and passed through any number of mail servers (also known as mail transfer agents, or MTAs) before it reaches its final destination.

Also, MTAs typically have a timeout set, so if a file does not make it through the gateway within a certain amount of time, it is left in the queue until the server is able to deliver it again later. In this way, a message can remain in the queue for several hours before any error is generated. Some mail servers have a 1 MB limit on message size, which means your message might not get through at all. Meanwhile, you are sitting around waiting, none the wiser. Email was not meant to go through these sorts of contortions. Don't rest your business on it.

A much better way of transferring files is to establish an FTP (File Transfer Protocol) site. FTP was designed specifically for the task of transferring files, especially large files, across the Internet. Because FTP calls for direct interaction between the client's machine and your server, it does not place as much of a load on any intermediary servers as email does. Also, the file is transferred in one piece, in one transfer session. At no time does it sit idle in a queue.

Unfortunately, using FTP is a little more complicated than attaching a file to an email message. To use an FTP site, you have to launch an FTP client, and enter a hostname, username, and password. Then you use the PUT command to transfer a local file to the remote server. Because we cannot assume that every client contact is familiar with these procedures, Adjacency has set up a web-based interface to our FTP site (see Figure 2.10). This enables client contacts to use a web browser to upload files in a familiar environment. This interface also enables us to include instructions in an easily readable format so that the transfer goes smoothly.

Figure 2.10

To simplify the collection of files from clients and vendors, Adjacency has designed a simple—yet effective—web-based FTP interface, complete with simplified platform-specific instructions for Mac, Windows, and Unix.

After the transfer is completed, Adjacency is notified that a file has been received. The task of verifying the transferred file and reviewing its contents is routed to the project leader for the client who performed the upload.

For more information on the specifics of using this web-based FTP interface for your own needs, please visit the companion site for this book at `http://www.adj.com/killer/`.

ORGANIZE AND GROUP CONTENT AREAS

Now that you have all this information from your client, what do you do with it? How do you organize it? No problem. Earlier in this chapter, we discussed how to identify your target audience's needs and expectations, which were broken down into the following categories—information, news, interaction, entertainment, and free stuff. This section talks about taking these general elements and grouping them into distinct identifiable and intuitive content areas. At the root of any web site, there are certain fundamental content areas that are usually incorporated in the site structure. Not all of these may be relevant for every site; the following list, however, offers an overview or sampling of common content areas that users tend to expect, as well as readily identify and use.

♦ **About the company**: People are curious about the company background and history. They want to know exactly what the company does, what kind of people work there, who runs the show, who builds the products, and so on. These kinds of details provide users with a clear picture of what the company is all about. Those unfamiliar with the company's products want to know about the company to determine the credibility of the products.

♦ **Product information**: People naturally expect comprehensive and detailed information about the web site's "product." Whether your site is about selling cars or saving rainforests in South America, you need areas on your site that provide information about your product, program, service, or event. If you are promoting software, people want to know the product features, system requirements, updates, and costs. They might also want to see a gallery of examples as well as tips on how to use the product. In the end, site visitors might want to know where to get or purchase the products, in which case you could provide an intelligent dealer locator or even an online store.

♦ **News/Press releases**: When people take the time to consider what your site has to offer, they want to know what's new, what's happening today, what developments and progress will occur, and what the rest of the world thinks about your company and products. Having a section on your site that deals with new items and announcements keeps users informed.

♦ **Frequently asked questions**: One way to organize information about your site and about the products is to come up with a page of frequently asked questions or FAQ. In the context of a question and answer format, users can have a directed point of reference in navigating through your site. Some people may not know what they want, much less where to start within your site. An FAQ furnishes users with ideas about how to deal with various issues regarding the site or product.

♦ **Contact information**: When all is said and done, your visitors need a way to get in touch with you because they invariably have questions about the web site or the company's products. Providing an email address, mailing address, telephone, and fax numbers sends a message to your customers that you care about what's on their minds.

In order to come up with logical section titles, you must walk through the proposed web site as a consumer, a site manager, and a marketing person would. You must consider how the end user would expect the information to be organized, while thinking about how the site is maintained. There usually is a compromise in organizing the content. Designing a web site is an eternal give and take between what the consumer wants and what the production team has to do in order to fulfill those expectations.

Here are the issues involved:

◆ **Graphic design**: You will be faced with the real estate challenge of making things fit visually in limited space. In Chapter 3, "Designing Web Site Aesthetics," the specifics in designing for the web are discussed. For now, keep in mind that you most likely have a great deal of text and graphics to fit in a 640×480 window. You need to select the appropriate typefaces, font sizes, color palettes, and graphics effects that best convey the brand identity in a clear, compelling, and organized interface.

◆ **Communication**: You must come up with section titles that make sense and that your audience can easily understand and identify. It is often dangerous to become too attached to cute, clever, and sexy names for sections. Does it really make sense to call the clothing line section of a fashion web site "The Rack" when all you mean is "The Clothes?" Probably not. In Chapter 4, we discuss the advantages and disadvantages of using metaphors. It is also especially dangerous to become locked into certain nomenclature that is not flexible enough to accommodate future information that doesn't fit within your original categories. You need to be focused and directed, but bend enough to make sure that everything makes sense within the context of how you have organized your site.

◆ **Site structure**: You must determine how to make the web site manageable and expandable. Assuming that you want and need your site to grow in the future, you need to prepare yourself for section name changes, deletions, and most likely additions. Vertical navigation works bests for sections or entire sites that will definitely have new items in the near future. If you create the perfect horizontal navigation bar that works excellently with six items, what will you do when you have three more items that must be added two months down the road? Redesign the whole navigational system? Good luck!

◆ **Marketing and branding**: Despite the concerns listed here, you may have to give way to the fact that your client has final say over the end result. Certain divisions within the client company might demand exposure of certain sections even though it may not make the most sense. The client may insist that somewhat obscure section names are used for branding purposes. An excellent way to compensate is to use tag lines placed beneath or nearby the section titles that describe in as few words as possible—and in as generic words as possible—what is contained within the section. Let's say, for instance, your client is a software company who insists on naming a section "Alpha Gold" after a technology partnership program open to third-party developers. A helpful title and subtitle could be "Alpha Gold: Developer Partnerships," or perhaps you may want to use a question to pique their interest: "Alpha Gold: Are you a developer?" Subtitles become especially valuable in sites forced to group large amounts of information within single sections to prevent users from being overwhelmed by an endless list of initial site options.

Thus, several considerations and layers of information can go into the creation of one web page.

When you have your section designations finalized, you are ready to begin creating a site map. A site map is essentially a flowchart outlining where content will fall in place as well as the hierarchical relationships between content areas. It's a great tool to help your production team as well as help your client understand how the site unfolds.

To construct a site map, use a flowchart program such as Org Plus that enables you to easily add and remove items as well as change the relationships between them (see Figure 2.11). See our appendix of tools and resources to learn more about this application.

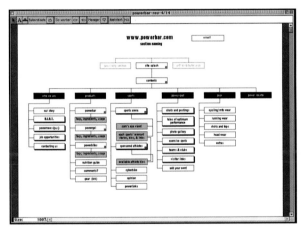

Figure 2.11

A handful of useful site map/flowchart generation programs exists on the market, including Org Plus, used here to create a preliminary PowerBar.com site map.

The PowerBar site map, for example, was set up with the splash (welcome) page at the top and the site menu directly below. Linked off of the site menu are the site's major content areas: Who We Are, Products, Sports, and so on. Then, linked off of each of these major content areas are the subsections contained within (under Who We Are there is the PowerBar Story, Employment Opportunities, and so on, for example).

It is useful to create a visual system to help clarify your site map. Some pages are accessible from every page on the site, such as email contact forms. For those, simply display them as a floating item off to the side of the site menu. For password-protected or hidden areas, try linking them with a dotted line. Also, adding a drop shadow under subsections that contain multiple pages helps to convey that there is a group of pages contained within.

The importance of using file naming conventions in building a web site cannot be understated, especially when dealing with large corporate web sites comprised of hundreds or even thousands of files. Naming conventions, when properly devised, can greatly ease the load of creating and maintaining any web site, small or large.

There is no hard-and-fast set of rules for discerning the naming conventions that should be used for any given web site. The naming conventions used should be developed with the specific objectives of your web site in mind and should be tailored to the peculiarities of your organization and its work habits.

Given this, here are some guidelines you may find helpful in approaching the task of developing a naming convention for your next big site.

THE ZEN OF INHERENT GROUPING

The first step in devising a naming convention is to determine exactly what it is you have to name. If, for example, you are building a site for a company that sells widgets and gadgets, you might choose to differentiate between those two groups of products in your filenames. By doing so, you can glance at any file and know right away if it is a photo of a widget or a gadget without opening the file.

Obviously you are likely to be dealing with a site that has far more than two categories. Indeed, client materials often seem beyond categorization, and they rarely come all together in a nice pretty package. Some files arrive as email attachments; some come on a CD-ROM from the client's service bureau (complete with its own alien naming scheme); some are uploaded to an FTP site by the client directly. The important thing is to use your intuition in discerning how the items relate to each other. Try to see beyond the content of an individual file in choosing its name; try to think about its relationship to the other files in the site. Ideally, you would be able to hold up all the files in your hands, let them fall through your fingers, and see where they land. Of course, it's never quite that easy.

In addition to the task of naming materials from the client, you must also account for the associated files you create for each piece of client collateral. For every page there will likely be a headline graphic; for every photo, a caption; for every section, a link GIF. Each of these must also be subjected to categorization.

CREATING A STANDARD SET OF PREFIXES AND SUFFIXES

Once you have a clear idea of the materials in front of you and how they relate to each other, it's time to get down to the nitty-gritty of naming. Let's return to our example company that makes widgets and gadgets. Suppose it makes each of these wonderful products in a variety of colors and sizes. You can buy a 3-inch red gadget or a 12-inch blue widget. Given this, it might be advisable to break your grouping into subgroups:

Widgets	Gadgets
3-inch	**3-inch**
red	red
blue	blue
green	green
yellow	yellow
6-inch	**6-inch**
red	red
blue	blue
green	green
yellow	yellow
12-inch	**12-inch**
red	red
blue	blue
green	green
yellow	yellow

Examining this, we see that for each product, there are three possible sizes, and for each size there are four possible colors. But how do we condense all this information into a single filename? The best way is to use prefixes and suffixes to indicate the identifying characteristics of a given file. Let's look at a 3-inch red widget as an example. It seems safe to assume that the file begins with the phrase "widget." The size can be abbreviated to "3in," whereas the color is pretty good as it is. If we put all this together, separated by underscores, we get "widget_3in_red." If we are dealing with a photo of a 3-inch red widget, we could call the whole thing "widget_3in_red_photo.jpg." (Note that it is generally unadvisable to use spaces in filenames on a web site. You can replace spaces with hyphens or underscores. At Adjacency, we usually use the latter.

Following this convention, a list of filenames for photos of the products listed above might look something like this:

widget_3in_red_photo.jpg
widget_3in_blue_photo.jpg
widget_3in_green_photo.jpg
widget_3in_yellow_photo.jpg
widget_6in_red_photo.jpg

widget_6in_green_photo.jpg
widget_6in_blue_photo.jpg
widget_6in_yellow_photo.jpg
and so on.

Although this enables us to easily predict what we might find in a given file, these filenames are a bit on the long side. Even if you feel comfortable working with such long filenames, this might not always be an option.

WORKING WITHIN THE LIMITATIONS OF YOUR FILE SYSTEM

Ideally, the length of the filenames you use in building a site would not be an issue. The maximum length of a filename, however, can vary greatly depending on the platform you choose for site development. Machines running DOS or Windows 3.1, for example, are limited to only eight-character names with a three-character file type extension, whereas some Unix file systems enable over 1,000 characters in a single filename.

At Adjacency, most of our development is done on MacOS and Windows 95 computers that support 31- and 255-character filenames, respectively, whereas the finished sites are served on a Unix machine that enables up to 1,024 characters. To accommodate this variety of platforms in naming our files, we have to limit ourselves to 31 characters, the greatest common denominator. Fortunately, this is usually enough to meet our needs.

If you are limited to a smaller number of characters, you need to be a little more frugal than the preceding filenames. Look for ways you can further shorten the filenames by abbreviating certain descriptors. In the preceding example, you might choose to abbreviate the part of the name that describes the color to one character because each color begins with a different letter. You could also abbreviate "photo" to "pho," lose the underscores, and abbreviate the phrases "widget" and "gadget."

If you are really short on space, you may want to use directories to help augment your naming conventions. Create a "widget" directory and a "gadget" directory, for example. By placing the widgets and gadgets in their respective folders, we eliminate the need to include this information in the filenames themselves. You might further subdivide the files by color and size or whatever attributes apply. Even if you have no limitations of filename length, you might want to use directories in this manner; they greatly facilitate organization and make for fewer headaches in the long run.

WORKING WITH A TEAM

All of this may seem like overkill if you work on your sites alone, but implementing a universal set of naming conventions is an indispensable practice when working with a team of developers. As soon as a project comes in the door, it's important to start this process in your head and to discuss it among those building the site. Create a project-specific mailing list and use it to keep everyone up to date with how filenames are being used throughout the site. Create a short white paper so that new people joining the project can quickly get a feel for how the site is organized.

Even if you are working alone, naming conventions can help you maintain your sanity, especially when working on large sites. If you have to leave a project and come back to it later, you will thank yourself for not having to figure out what the heck all those cryptic filenames mean.

DIRECT VISITOR FLOW

In designing the navigational structure of a site, you want to keep the visitor's questions in mind at all times. When they reach the site, they are likely to ask themselves: What is here for me? How do I find what I am looking for? How does all this information relate to me? It is your responsibility to answer these questions for them, and to point them in the right directions from the start.

Although you want a web site to maintain an open feel that encourages the user to explore, you do not want the site to feel chaotic or unorganized. Make it clear to the user that the information he or she is looking for is available and that it is in the place they would expect to find it. Assure the user that you have done the dirty work of organizing the information for him or her.

When you want to drive visitors to certain areas of a site, there are various strategies you can use. The most common of these is to feature a link in a prominent position. An extreme example of this is the NeXT home page during the Apple-NeXT merger, which at the time featured a link to information about the merger that filled approximately 80 percent of the page. This strategy made sense because that was by far the most sought after information on their site for several weeks.

Another option is to redirect users to the content you want them to see after they reach a "stopping point" in the navigational structure of the site. Lufthansa created a sweepstakes in order to draw users to their site, for example. After filling out the sweepstakes entry form, visitors were presented with an overview of the rest of the site, with links to major content areas. This increased awareness of the information available on the site. We talk more about this particular strategy in Chapter 4.

Whatever strategy you choose, make sure that when visitors reach your site their options are clear to them and that it is up to them to decide where they want to go.

Following from this, you should make it easy for users to move around within your site. You have a responsibility of providing information to your audience compellingly, easily, and quickly. If you enable users to cross-navigate between and within sections of your web site, you reduce the number of screens and reloads between your visitor and the information that they want.

You can achieve cross-navigability by providing consistent site navigation through:

- ◆ **Graphics**: When people see a common graphic or visual clue in the same placement on different web pages, they can orient themselves more easily. They understand that they are in the same environment of your site when they see these graphics. In general, graphics are the most easily identifiable means for someone to recognize your site. Users may remember the text content, but they will definitely remember cool graphics (see Figure 2.12).

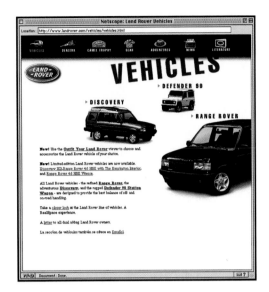

Figure 2.12

The Land Rover site uses horizontal and vertical navigation bars to enable the user to move from section to section. The navigation bar is horizontal on the site menu and on the main page of each section, but once the user moves into a content area, the navigation moves to the side, enabling the content to take precedence. Notice that the current section is always highlighted in red.

◆ **Frames**: Placing your navigational links, whether they are hypertext links or an imagemap, in a frame enables users to peruse the content of the site without ever losing their way back to the other sections.

Although they might be scrolling up and down content pages, the navigational frame remains fixed. The navigational links never scroll away (see Figure 2.13).

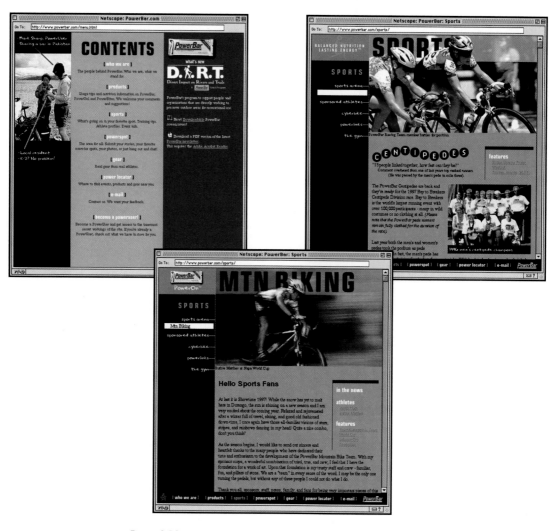

Figure 2.13

When you delve into the content of the PowerBar site, a bottom frame enables easy navigation between sections. A frame on the side also facilitates navigation within each section.

◆ **Search Engine**: Although a search mechanism on your site enables users to go directly to their desired information, the design elements mentioned earlier give them the option to navigate freely between the sections (see Figure 2.14).

Figure 2.14

Because the Kemper site contains so much information, a search engine is used to complement its navigational scheme. There is a search link on every page. Keyword searches generate ranked, hyperlinked lists of relevant pages and content areas.

Although users get to reap the benefits of cross-navigability, you are faced with the challenge of implementing this consistent design throughout several pages. What happens when you copy and paste HTML code on 40 different pages to include a specific list of hypertext links, only to find out afterwards that you need to change the name of one of the sections? The following sidebar covers server-side includes that enable you to manage your HTML editing more easily. Instead of changing 40 files, you only have to change one!

EASE YOUR LOAD WITH SERVER-SIDE INCLUDES

Although the ability to cross-navigate from any page in a site is definitely a plus, it can also add a lot of work to the development and maintenance of the site. Changing one text link in your navigation scheme means changing it in dozens or even hundreds of files. Doing this by hand can be tedious and increases the likelihood of errors. You certainly have better things to do with your time. Using server-side includes, you can leave some of this work to your computer.

A server-side include is a command inserted in your HTML that the server reads and executes before sending the HTML to the user. The results of the command are inserted, or included, in place of the command. A simple include looks like this:

```
<!--#INCLUDE FILE="navigation.incl"-->
```

This tells the server to find the file navigation.incl (in the same directory as the HTML file) and insert its contents in place of the include command (see Figure 2.15). By adding this command to all the pages in a section and then storing the HTML snippet that defines the navigation for that section in the include file, you can make site updates a breeze. Make a change in the include file and it is automatically reflected in any documents that use that include.

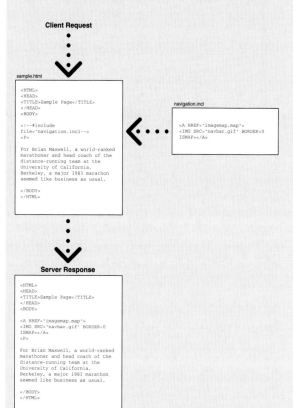

Figure 2.15

When the user requests a page that contains a server-side include, the server replaces the include statement with the text stored in the include file and sends the composited document back to the user.

There are some caveats to be aware of before using this tool. First of all, not all server software is capable of using server-side includes. Some server software supports it in a limited capacity. Check with your system administrator to find out if (and to what degree) your server software supports server-side includes.

Another disadvantage is that using server-side includes increases the load on your server. When the server has to look for the include file and insert its contents, processing time for each HTTP request increases. Depending on the processor speed of your server, this can translate to slower response times for your end users. Most newer hardware can handle the load with little or no problem. You have to decide who needs more work: you or your server?

There is a lot more that can be done with server-side includes than what is illustrated here. For more information on server-side includes, visit NCSA's tutorial at `http://hoohoo.ncsa.uiuc.edu/docs/tutorials/includes.html`.

An added feature you might want to include on your site is a search engine feature. Some people simply prefer to go directly to the search area of a site to find exactly what they are looking for. These people are not necessarily interested in browsing through your site no matter how well designed and cutting-edge the layouts may be. We have included another sidebar that discusses how to build a search engine into your site.

BUILDING A SEARCH ENGINE INTO YOUR SITE

One of the nicest things you can do for users is ensure that they have little trouble finding what they're looking for when they come to your site. To this end, it is important that the information on your site is divided into clear, logical groups, and that the navigation and directory structure of your site reflects this organization. Taking these precautions is often all it takes to make it easier for your users to find what they need quickly and easily.

If, however, you are building a large site with lots of detailed, subject-specific content that changes frequently, it may be imperative to take further measures to increase the users' ability to find the information they desire. If this is the case, you may want to consider building a search engine into your site. This enables users to enter a few keywords and quickly scan the titles of pages that contain that keyword.

In order to do this, you need to take some preliminary steps so that your site is easily searchable by the engine. When building the Bicycle Guide site, we took advantage of the little-used <META> tag to insert descriptive information at the beginning of each document:

```
<HEAD>
<TITLE>Bicycle Guide: Road Test: KHS Aero
Turbo</TITLE>
<META name="section" content="Road Tests
and First Rides">
<META   name="post-date"   content="96-09-
01">
</HEAD>
```

The search engine scans the entire site once a day, creating an index containing a reference to every page in the site. Accompanying each page reference is the section name and date gathered from its <META> tags, as well as all the non-HTML text found in the body of the page.

When the user performs a search, the engine checks the index for all occurrences of the keyword in the body text for each page. It then returns a list of matching pages, showing the title, section name, and post date.

The engine used for the Bicycle Guide was custom-built by Adjacency. Explaining its inner workings is beyond the scope of this book. If you want to add a search engine to your site, have a look at the freeware search engine provided by Excite at http://www.excite.com/navigate.

SUMMARY

Creating an effective web site that communicates a clear message about your client and appeals to specific target audiences depends on having a rock-solid plan. Before starting the production of a web site, you need to make a list of objectives with a matching set of strategies to accomplish those goals. These strategies involve knowing the users and organizing the site architecture. If you understand exactly who the target audience is and what their needs are, you can create a web site that meets and perhaps surpasses your client's objectives. Because you have dedicated yourself to developing a clear user profile, you will be able to *anticipate* your users' needs and make informed decisions about what web aesthetics and interactive features to design in the production phase.

CHAPTER 3

IN THE PREVIOUS CHAPTER, WE SHOWED YOU HOW TO CREATE SECTION DESIGNATIONS IN RELATION TO THE BRAND IDENTITY AND MESSAGE. THIS CHAPTER GUIDES YOU THROUGH THE PROCESS OF VISUALIZING THESE AREAS AND CREATING AN INTUITIVE INTERFACE THAT DISTINGUISHES THE AREAS WITHIN YOUR SITE NAVIGATIONAL SYSTEM. A WELL-DESIGNED SITE GIVES USERS FEEDBACK **DESIGNING WEB** ABOUT WHERE THEY **SITE** ARE **AESTHETICS** IN RELATION TO THE OTHER LAYERS OF CONTENT WITHIN THE SITE. IN A SENSE, THE ENTIRE SITE INTERFACE REPRESENTS AN ABSTRACT SITE MAP. REMEMBER THAT AESTHETICS INVOLVE MORE THAN ART FOR ART'S SAKE. YOU MAY CERTAINLY CREATE EXPANSIVE, BEAUTIFUL GRAPHICS WITH FANCY TONES, GRADIENTS, AND SPECIAL EFFECTS, BUT IF THE FILE SIZE AMOUNTS TO MORE THAN WHAT YOUR USER'S BANDWIDTH CAN HANDLE REASONABLY, YOU LOSE YOUR AUDIENCE'S ATTENTION AND SUBSEQUENTLY THE AUDIENCE. SIMILARLY, IF THE STYLE OR NATURE OF THE GRAPHIC DIVERGES FROM THE BRAND'S IDENTITY, YOU WEAKEN THE STRENGTH OF ONE CONSISTENT MESSAGE. AS WITH ANY FORM OF GOOD DESIGN, A WELL-CRAFTED WEB SITE REINFORCES AND COMMUNICATES A SPECIFIC MESSAGE WITH A DISTINCTIVE FLAIR THAT SHOULD NOT GET IN THE WAY OF THE SITE'S FUNCTIONALITY AND PURPOSE.

This chapter discusses the big picture behind designing web aesthetics. We guide you through the different issues you must take into consideration as you approach the drawing board. Although the immediacy of the web and rapidly evolving technologies place a great deal of pressure on designers and developers to create and update their sites quickly, you must stop and think carefully about your client's needs and objectives in light of the basic design principles that result in a successful web interface.

How to reinforce your client's corporate identity on the web is addressed in this chapter. We help you overcome the distraction of web technology to create sites that are consistent in message and quality with your client's existing identity system. You learn how to practice basic fundamentals that exercise and tone your design muscles and whip your design sense into shape! This chapter encourages you to create web aesthetics that transcend anything you have seen. You won't be limited by the technology or existing web practices. We also walk you through the process of designing a web interface—from graphics preparation and optimization to page layout. Finally, you are provided with a comprehensive checklist to tighten up the design and portability of your web site across different platforms and browsers.

MAINTAINING YOUR CLIENT'S CORPORATE IDENTITY ON THE WEB

By this time, you should have already taken a step back to synthesize all of the information about your client's brand, objectives, and strategies, as well as information about the web as a design medium and communication tool. Such information helps to remind you about the issues discussed earlier in "Evaluating the Brand" and "Developing Site Strategy and Structure." Far too often, the nitty-gritty details of the end result of a design can absorb and preoccupy someone working on as grand an endeavor as building a web site. Remember that your site must be clear, concise, and compelling in order for it to be useful to an audience. In order to achieve these qualities, you must always keep a clear picture in mind of your client's corporate identity, brand strategy, and web site objectives.

Adjacency was started two years ago in reaction to the rampant misinterpretation of company and brand images in relation to their respective web sites. On top of the notion that many sites missed the mark, they also appeared unprofessional and insufficiently designed, as if an amateur had assembled them. The sites seemed inauthentic. Today, an increasing percentage of Adjacency projects involve complete redesigns due to others' failures in representing the client and communicating the brand image and message.

Many early corporate web sites were created by entirely technology-driven web development companies whose pioneering work attested to their programming ability, but whose graphic design was often lacking. Logos—images in general— were often poorly rendered and randomly or uninspiringly placed. Most troubling, many early corporate web sites shared no visual consistency with the client companies' concurrent print and broadcast efforts. Unfortunately, subsequent finger-pointing often singled out companies' IS managers' insensitivity to corporate design standards and branding in general as the culprit. That attitude is over-simplified and flawed. It is an attitude that unfairly absolves marketing people and graphic designers of their responsibility to stay abreast of emerging communications technologies. In short, graphic designers fell asleep at the wheel.

OBSERVE YOUR CLIENT'S CORPORATE DESIGN STANDARDS

In a medium such as the web, where a company's corporate communications literally bleed into other companies' (online) collateral, the importance of corporate identity standards are especially acute. Your client's site visitor is always only a few links from the "outside." Strong, identifiable, and consistent use of your client's corporate identity elements reminds and reassures site visitors where they are at all times.

Your client's logotype and symbol(s) are among your most potent, recognizable, and authoritative visual cues. Needless to say, you must observe all corporate standards when rendering and displaying them and integrating them into layouts. As a digital medium, the web affords designers more instantaneous and transformative freedom in creating graphics. With the click of a mouse or the typing of a quick key, you're able to change the color or scale the size of a logo or symbol. When you're translating a company's corporate identity to the web, you must practice restraint. Stick with the tried and true. Resist the urge—often the client's urge—to reinvent a perfectly good, well-recognized brand for the web in some MTV-esque, cyber-this, cyber-that, tech-savvy version of its former self. There should be a special suburb in Hell reserved for web developers who make non-spherical corporate logotypes spin.

Many companies have found a way to integrate a consistently placed company logo functionally into a site's navigational scheme. By linking the logo in each instance to the main site menu or front end of a site, you can call further attention to the logotype and make an otherwise compulsory corporate ID element earn its real estate on the page. What's more, on some Pavlovian plane, using the corporate logo for navigation simply makes brand exposure sense to entice visitors to click the logo or symbol—and see a result—whenever possible (see Figure 3.1).

Figure 3.1

The Lufthansa logo is consistently sized and rendered throughout the site. Linked to the site directory, it serves as a key navigational element.

CREATING ONLINE CORPORATE DESIGN STANDARDS

Lufthansa-USA.com successfully demonstrates how well-established corporate design standards can be maintained on the web without diminishing the boldness or uniqueness of the finished product. Designed to reinforce the upscale Lufthansa brand to web-savvy, affluent American Transatlantic business travelers, the Lufthansa-USA web site combines clean typography, well-reasoned navigation and vivid photography—international-style design sans web gimmicks. The site maintains the brand with efficiency and elegance and though decidedly interactive and "tech," Lufthansa-USA.com does not wear its programming on its sleeve.

Lufthansa's web site was a challenging project because the company has very strict corporate design guidelines.

We were required to use only Helvetica type throughout the site, for instance; a restriction we used to our advantage. In the HTML <FONT> tag, we specified Helvetica and/or Helvetica-derived fonts (Arial and Geneva) so that the default bitmapped Times on most browsers would be overridden and replaced with the bitmapped counterpart to the clean, anti-aliased Helvetica headline and link images on the page. That gave the site a sort of typographic unity/consistency rarely afforded sites whose headlines are rendered in typefaces with no bitmapped, operating system font facsimiles (see Figure 3.2).

 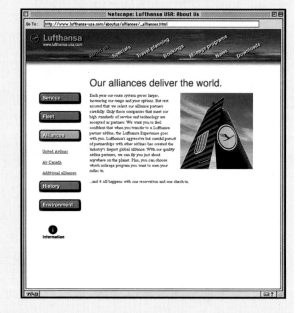

Figure 3.2

By being able to specify Helvetica-derived proportional fonts to display hypertext, designers were able to maintain Lufthansa's corporate type standards online (left). The end result is much more stylistically unified than the same page with the more common browser default font, Times (right).

We also had a limited color palette to work with: blue, dark gray, light gray, black, and white. Again, the best way to deal with limitations is to make them "features." Solid background colors were chosen from the palette to color-code different levels of the site. The result is a site that gets a lighter, more open feel as you go deeper, transforming from first black to dark gray to white. Light gray was avoid-ed entirely because of its historic associations with old-school browsers and first-generation web sites (although light gray has been replaced recently by white as the no-brainer background color of unconscious choice). The blues were reserved for the top cross-navigational header bar. It tied together visually all of the levels in the site and contrasted nicely with the more hue-neutral colors used for level backgrounds (see Figure 3.3).

 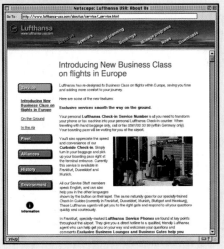

Figure 3.3

Lufthansa-USA.com uses the company's corporate colors to create a progression from the darker, high-level pages to the white background, content-rich lower-level pages. Color-coded site strata give users a visual clue as to where they are in a site.

Lufthansa's corporate multimedia design standards also dictated that the navigational scheme was based on arrays of labeled buttons. The trick to using buttons properly is that you need to use and position them 100% consistently. The second you accidentally add variation, you destroy all visual credibility. Buttons add a mechanical feel/metaphor to an interface and therefore need to be handled regimentally. We made sure to place them within a rigid grid within the same area on each page. This fanatically consistent placement also aids the visitor in navigation. After the first couple pages, the visitor knows instinctively where to click. Sounds simple, but when users hit a page for the first time, they are forced to learn a new way to navigate. Flagrant variation within a site can be confusing. Adjacency rarely uses buttons in its interface design, but Lufthansa-USA.com offered us an interesting opportunity to get that approach right (see Figure 3.4).

In general, we were discouraged from using non-photographic illustrations, aside from line-drawn diagrams. Realizing we had a site whose general color scheme and typography weren't exactly the most expressive, we saw photos as a way to humanize the site. The richest, most emotional and colorful images were sought out. The contrast and colors were bumped up a bit, to get that especially deep, rich look.

One other rule regarding photo use was that we were not allowed to silhouette images; they all had to be rectangularly cropped. There was only one opportunity where it made sense to work around this restriction: the main menu page. We wanted to create the (not entirely literal or photorealistic) reference to being in an airplane looking out, so a dark photo shot from a seat in a Lufthansa plane was used. The lighting made the bulkhead

surrounding the window very dark, almost black. We pushed the dark areas of the interior of the plane all the way to black so the image would blend seamlessly into the main menu page's black background. The image introduced the site using an apt metaphor that immediately implied to people, "Get prepared to catch a flight compliments of Lufthansa." The results were visually stunning enough to win us the nod from the corporate standards people. As a side note, the design was also intended to enable us to path-in new sky shots in the window area, enabling an interestingly subtle way of refreshing the front end every so often.

Figure 3.4

Luftahansa's corporate new media design standards required Adjacency to use standardized button images for links within the Lufthansa-USA.com web site. By being extremely consistent with the placement of the button arrays, we used the requirement to make navigation as easy as possible.

Another minor standards victory we won was to be allowed to create a top cross-navigation array in the interface that, instead of using buttons, used diagonally rotated type. We believed this type added a nice sense of angularity and movement to what otherwise might have been an oppressively perpendicular layout. The way the diagonal elements complement the lines of the airplane window on the site menu page especially pleased us.

Our ultimate aesthetic goal for the site was to combine all of the site design elements to create a rich, substantial-looking site that reflected the quality and precision of our client and its services. The site needed to reinforce Lufthansa-USA's existing and highly recognizable corporate identity and design standards while embracing yet another visual communications medium. We feel we succeeded.

At times, you may have to work with your client's internal design department. Although adding more people to a project can complicate the production process, you can make the situation work to your advantage. Your client brings you into the picture because you are the web expert. The client's designers are most likely print designers with little or no web experience. Coming from the outside, you can give a fresh perspective to the site, and the internal designers can critique your web designs with no self-editing or limitations. These designers will ask tough questions that you will have to justify, questions that help you examine your own process.

USE YOUR IMAGINATION AND COMMON SENSE

Though the starting point of many web sites stems from existing corporate identity materials, you should challenge yourself to come up with totally new and fresh ways to present the information. Take the material out of context and reexamine it through the eyes of a web audience. Rarely do we want to take a page out of our clients' print pieces and reconstruct them on the web, unless it's an annual report where the predictability of the layout plays a significant role in users' expectations. As we've shown with the Land Rover case study in Chapter 1, blindly copying and repurposing print material, although easy and straightforward, may not address the client's web audience properly.

Often, maintaining a client's corporate identity on the web involves simply imagining, "If Company X had a web site, what would it look like? What colors do I see? What pictures do I see? What typefaces would I expect?" Your answers to these questions pinpoint the essence of the client's image as well as support the information you gathered from evaluating the brand.

Therefore, consider the given print materials as guides, not rules, in your web design plans. You do not always base the project solely on what the client gives you. An entire visual system of colors, fonts, graphic materials, and section hierarchies will be created by you especially for the web site. At the same time, you should not diverge completely from the style or feeling of the existing corporate identity. The transition from traditional media to the web should be as seamless as possible. Whatever you do needs to reinforce the company so that the web site doesn't look like it came from a different company.

Even if you do not have effective, existing materials with which to work and you must start from scratch, you need to make sure that the resulting web site looks like it belongs to the client company. Each corporate communications and marketing piece for a company defines its brand message and identity. A web site is no exception. Just because you can provide a fresh, new perspective to the treatment of a product through the web does not entitle you to create something totally unrelated to the original message. The Rollerblade case study in this section offers some helpful insights on how to deal with a project where you must start from scratch.

ROLLERBLADE: STARTING FROM SCRATCH

When we began working with Rollerblade, the company was in the midst of a major brand review. Over the past few years Rollerblade had used many vendors to create its printed, broadcast, and promotional merchandise, point of sale materials, and packaging (see Figure 3.5). Every year a different company was used to do the catalog, which meant that there was probably a different style used each time. The Rollerblade image was not focused. The company approached us with the challenge to take inventory of what it had done in the past to set out for a newer, more refined, concentrated direction.

Figure 3.5
A grouping of some of Rollerblade's older print collateral shows the various visual styles the company had assumed over a short period of time.

As with any client, in trying to find the soul of Rollerblade we sat down and reviewed all of its corporate communication pieces. We strove to create a site that seamlessly integrated the look and feel from the existing materials to the web medium. In this case, we were sitting there with a pile of brochures whose styles and attitude did not fit with each other. There was no continuity. On top of that, we were told that Rollerblade was going to do something totally different—something that it had not even created yet.

Why didn't we wait to create the site? Because Rollerblade saw the web site as an important initiative that would serve as one of the first new design efforts. Our client was the Rollerblade public relations director, who saw the web site as a corporate communications tool. Rollerblade was updating and refocusing itself, and it wanted us to help with the reinvention. The web would be the instrument to facilitate these new initiatives.

What did we do? What did we have? Not having any printed material that would tell us where we were going, we turned to the most obvious thing: inline skating. Our goal, as described earlier, was to create the definitive online skating site. By creating a site that represented both the sport and the company, we would establish a design that could withstand different changes developed during the brand review process.

There were probably safer ways to do what we did with the Rollerblade site, but we didn't just want to create an all right, okay site—a site with no strong visuals and no character. Instead we went for boldness and excitement without any design gimmicks that would be outdated in three months (see Figure 3.6). We simply wanted to push the envelope with pumped-up images that would stop people from talking about web pages and start them talking about web posters.

The archetypal web page, with its small images and overwhelming white space, seems at its best uninspiring; its worst, chintzy. Also, many pages designed as a composite of multiple images seem disjointed, newspaper-like. The Rollerblade site boasts large-scale pages dominated—*unified*—by single, full-bleed images. What's more, many web pages use color sparingly, possibly because the people who design them, coming from print

backgrounds, are accustomed to printing on white- or light-colored paper stocks. On the web, color is next to free. Rollerblade was poised to take advantage of that.

Figure 3.6
Adjacency designed Rollerblade.com to celebrate and fixate upon the sport. Large, dynamic action photography was to be king.

A consistent typography was used throughout the site to create a slightly edgy feel without making it too typeface-dependent. To reinforce movement within the content, we manipulated the type to create sharp angles and death-defying geometry. Type links and headlines were used so that they would interact with what was going on in the photos.

Figure 3.7

Adjacency combined stylized type with photographs on Rollerblade.com to create cohesive, unified page designs.

The photographs were key in creating bold statements. Because the shots we had were cropped vertically, we had to create the illusion of wider landscapes manually. Adobe Photoshop was used to add more sky, more clouds, more trees, more buildings, or more people. We also had to add, clone, and clean up images to make them fit the appropriate layout we were going for. Kenneth Greer and Associates in Minneapolis is a photo and design studio that has worked closely with Rollerblade and has done an excellent job in capturing lifestyle shots and sponsored athletes, whereas Mike Vorhees did the product shots. We were extremely lucky to have good photography to work with.

While creating our own tweaks and adjustments, we still had to make this site totally Rollerblade. How? We made sure that the product sections conveyed a clear and consistent message. When you look at a Rollerblade product page, you see skates blown up on a huge scale on bold color backgrounds. The scale and composition is kept consistent so that you understand you are still on the same bold site.

In addition to layout and stylistic consistencies, we adhered to consistent logo placement throughout the site. We also made the Rollerblade logo a navigational element that links back to the main site menu. By making the logo clickable, you make sure that people look at it and interact with it. Such small but prominent touches can add more brand awareness and value to your site.

As you can see, with a logo, some strong product shots, a strong design sense, and creativity, you can create a compelling and engaging site. Today, the Rollerblade site still attracts a large audience due to the informative content, clear and bold design, and the fast downloads.

PRACTICING GOOD DESIGN FUNDAMENTALS

Although effective design often produces a simple result, good design doesn't just happen. Successful designs result from careful consideration and an awareness of basic design fundamentals. In this section, we discuss the basics of consistency, clarity, expressiveness, and daring.

BE CONSISTENT

The problem with any poorly designed web site is inconsistency. As a web designer or developer, you must create your web site as a finite, predictable universe with a specific set of standards and design specifications. You need to make your pages believable within that scheme. When people go to any given page on your site, they should be able to recognize that they're in the same site, the same little world.

Because users can link between different pages of a single site and totally different sites, they need simple clues of where they are. Some visual hints involve using consistent typefaces for specific needs and consistent placement and layout. If you have text headers and subheadings, make sure that you use a consistent font size, style, and face for each scenario. Your graphics should also tie in together in such a way that seeing them in a sequence or as a whole does not appear disjointed or non-cohesive. Use consistent styles and color palettes. If you diverge from your rules in order to highlight something, make it deliberate and thoughtful. An area that demands extra, special attention can look distinctive, but it should still look related to the whole of your site. You need a reason for everything you do on the site.

Consistency results in simplicity, clarity, easy utility—qualities your users need and appreciate. You define the pattern your page layouts follow. Without a pattern, you are faced with a brand new design problem with each section of the site. Later on in this chapter we discuss the specifics of actually designing the interface and setting up a layout grid. For now, you should be aware that consistency is one of the keys to designing a successful and effective web site. Once you have this concept drilled into your brain, you can take advantage of HTML techniques that automate and organize consistency features of your site. One such method is using style sheets. The following sidebar deals with cascading style sheets to standardize the typefaces on your web pages.

WE HAVE SEEN THE FUTURE: CASCADING STYLE SHEETS

If you've spent any time at all building web pages, you've probably realized that HTML has many inherent limitations. You know that translating print design to the web can be difficult, impractical, or even impossible using even the best HTML tricks around. You know that site maintenance is always worse than you expected it to be, especially because making a change on one page often means making the same change on hundreds of other pages. You know that to do any "real" typography, you have to resort to using huge GIFs. And you know that if you get too crazy with your pages, using browser-specific HTML and relying heavily on graphic elements, you risk scaring away visitors.

If you know all these things, you should know one more thing: it doesn't have to be that way.

Having witnessed the outrageous things designers were attempting to do with HTML, the folks who established the HTML standard quickly set about developing a better means to allow designers to achieve the effects they wanted without bending all the rules. The result is a revolutionary concept known as Cascading Style Sheets.

Style sheets enable you to format your information using plain and simple HTML that any browser can read, while also enabling you to define rules that tell browsers how to render your code. As an example, let's create a simple document:

```
<HTML>
<HEAD>
<TITLE>In praise of style sheets</TITLE>
</HEAD>
<BODY>
<H1>CSS</H1>
<H3>cascading style sheets</H3>
<DIV CLASS=content>
<B>Imagine:</B><BR>
<BR>
No more single-pixel gifs<BR>
Cross-platform consistency<BR>
No more embedded tables<BR>
Easy site maintenance<BR>
More free time<BR>
</DIV>
</BODY>
</HTML>
```

When viewed in most present-day browsers, this code would look much like the page shown in Figure 3.8. Pretty boring, huh?

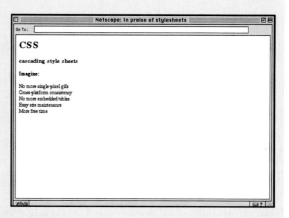

Figure 3.8

The history of design on the web is strewn with the corpses of bland, unexpressive pages.

If, however, you add a simple set of style rules at the beginning of this document, the browser of the future will know that this code should in fact look more like the page shown in Figure 3.9.

Figure 3.9

Cascading style sheets enable designers to create bolder, more typographically controlled and structurally compelling web pages without forcing them to resort to rendering type as images.

The difference is pretty dramatic. So what is this magic and how do you get your hands on it? Let's examine the style rules that we used to achieve this result:

```
<STYLE TYPE="text/css">
    <!--
  BODY { background: #669966; }
H1    { font: italic 200px Verdana, sans-
serif;
      color: white; }
H3    { font: bold 30px/14px Arial Black,
sans-serif;
      position: absolute;
      top: 100px; left: 150px;
      color: red;
      text-decoration: underline; }
.content { position: absolute; top: 75px;
left: 450px;
          font: 10px/30px Geneva; text-
decoration: underline; }
-->
</STYLE>
```

This information is inserted in the head of the document. Each rule consists of the name of an HTML tag followed by the characteristics you wish to assign to each instance of that tag. The <BODY> tag, for example, is defined as having a muted green background color. The <H1> tag is defined as using italic Verdana type, 200 pixels high. If Verdana is unavailable, the browser uses the default sans-serif font on the system, whatever that may be. These are but a few of the attributes you can define through style sheets.

Don't worry if the syntax seems unfamiliar to you; you should approach learning style sheets in the same way you approached learning HTML. Familiarize yourself with the general concepts and get a feel for how styles can be used for manipulating your HTML. When you have questions

about syntax, check out *Web Designer's Guide to Style Sheets* by Steven Mulder, published by Hayden Books, or refer to the W3C white paper at http://www.w3.org/pub/WWW/TR/REC-CSS1.

So why are they called Cascading Style Sheets? The term *cascading* refers to the various levels at which you can apply style sheets, which basically fall into three categories. You can apply a style at the elemental level, such as defining a style for a single tag; the document level, as we have in our example, defining a set of style rules throughout a certain document; and the site level, creating a separate style sheet document that defines styles for any HTML document that references your style sheet. This last example is where style sheets really come into their own. By applying styles site-wide from a single document, you can update your entire site instantly just by making changes to your master style sheet.

Powerful as style sheets are, it will still be some time before they can feasibly be used as the basis for building any site that needs to reach a wide audience. Style sheets are presently only implemented in Internet Explorer 3 and higher and Netscape Navigator 4, which is still in beta at the time of this writing. Furthermore, the implementation seems to differ slightly between the two browsers, but hopefully these kinks will work themselves out. Although it may seem like an annoyance waiting for CSS-capable browsers to become pervasive, you should view this time as an opportunity to master this new technology so that you'll be ready when the sheets hit the streets.

DON'T CROWD YOUR PAGES

Web content needs to be presented in digestible chunks. When you crowd your page—whether in the navigation and/or in the main content area—with too many elements, you cook up a recipe for visual vomit (a sickening image indeed!). A crowded page diffuses your message and consequently confuse and overwhelm your users (see Figure 3.10).

Figure 3.10

Lufthansa-USA.com features clean, uncluttered pages that present the user with very little superfluous information or graphical gimics.

The elements of your pages need to strike a balance between being zippy and fast. You need to organize the information visually so that the content appears friendly, neat, and approachable. You must organize your graphics and text to leave allowance for empty space and "breathing room." If your graphics and text run into each other with no apparent rhyme or reason, you don't give viewers a chance to absorb the information in reasonable segments. Even if you have just text on a page, you must deal with organizing the sentences into paragraphs and lists where individual characters and words look orderly and organized. Take

advantage of the `<BLOCKQUOTE>` and `<P>` tags to add buffers around your paragraphs. If you have a page with three `<H3>` headings individually stacked on top of three corresponding paragraphs, experiment with alternative ways to call out the headings and minimize the width of the paragraphs. Try placing the text in tables where headings are aligned in the left column and paragraphs are at the right. This kind of arrangement breaks up the sea of text into a clean organized arrangement.

BE EXPRESSIVE

While keeping your web page elements to a bare minimum, you must also strive to squeeze the most boldness and effect per kilobyte. We assemble things to hopefully evoke some emotion and character. If we make one page that makes people say, "Wow! This doesn't look like a web page. How did they do that?," then we know we've gone beyond the old-school web sites that strictly provide information in text. Remember that in designing a web site, you are not designing a newspaper or report. You are designing a poster.

Graphics serve as the most obvious and compelling vehicle for boldness and expressiveness. As the saying goes, "a picture is worth a thousand words." Only one compelling image is needed to deliver a strong message with punch on a page; not ten or twenty pictures (see Figure 3.11). Furthermore, graphics span a variety of forms—from a regular illustration or photograph to a web graphic used to demonstrate special typographical treatment. The following sections on "scrunching" images discuss the specifics on how to minimize the file sizes of your graphics without compromising the quality and character of the image.

Figure 3.11

The recent redesign of Rollerblade.com shows how high-impact page designs can make the added wait for large images to download worth your site visitors' time. But remember, it better be good.

At the same time, you can't achieve the same "Wow!" with random bells and whistles lumped together in an non-cohesive manner that only shows off technology for technology's sake. You need to think about the entire package of the web site you are presenting. Again, a good reason is needed for everything you do. Expressing yourself or communicating a client's message powerfully does not rely on cheap tricks. You need to be able to offer a solid and distinctive design with well-written text, compelling images, and useful features.

PUSH THE LIMITS OF YOUR DESIGN

Web sites need more passion. People don't push sites enough to unleash the potential energy that lies within the web as a visual communication medium. People need to get over their inhibitions about experimenting with new ideas.

Expressiveness doesn't mean cramming pages from edge to edge with text, pictures, assemblages of type and pictures, buttons, and logos. Web pages look like web pages because they are afraid to be empty. You can do so much with empty space to create unique, asymmetrical designs that bust out of the usual predictability of the TV dinner look of web page layouts (see Figure 3.12).

Figure 3.12

Exciting web pages surprise people. This Rollerblade product page, for example, visually conveys an awful lot about that brand's value long before immersing the reader in detailed product specs.

Many people are also afraid to use an implied rhythm in their web page designs. You don't need an animated GIF to suggest a sense of motion and movement. Angles and geometry can create a kinetic mood within your pages. Explore different options for orienting and aligning elements onscreen. Try tilting big titles. Cut the corners of your rectangular images or blurring the edges. In fact, try cropping your images down into alternative shapes such as circles, trapezoids, or stars. Try playing with the color balance in your graphics or creating a duotone look as opposed to a predictable snapshotty photograph.

Ask yourself and others questions about why certain approaches haven't been tried on the web, but don't accept the easy answers. Doubt. Test. Provoke. Don't just push the envelope, shred it. Eat the stamp. Read magazines such as Graphis, Print, ID, and Communication Arts. More importantly, look at the pictures. Hoard back issues like a junkie.

Admittedly, one of the most powerful forces pushing the rapid evolution of and experimentation within web design is print design. Web designers must be graphic designers first and foremost. They must stay abreast of what's going on and, perhaps as importantly, what has come to pass in other areas of design. In the way the desktop publishing revolution of the late '80s and early '90s made everyone a typographer, the web boom is fast making every digital production artist and computer animator a web designer. Though such a massive influx of people (at least in name) into the field brings with it excitement and innovation, the designers with knowledge of where design has been and where it's going will become even more valuable than they already are. When hiring, we at Adjacency have a conceit we mumble to ourselves like autistic headhunters: "Give us a phenomenal print designer and we'll teach him or her the fundamentals of designing for interactivity within two months. Teaching design and aesthetics takes a lot longer."

DESIGNING THE INTERFACE

Now that you have the initial theorizing, philosophizing, organizing, and planning out of the way,

you're ready to design! But before getting into production mode, you need to know exactly what you are designing. You are designing an interface for your web site, but what does that mean? According to the dictionary, an interface is "a surface forming a common boundary between adjacent regions."

In web speak, there are standard interface elements common to most sites. Here are the usual parts of a web interface:

- ◆ **Navigation**: Global, local, and regular hypertext links within the content that enable the user to jump between regions.
- ◆ **Section headers**: Indicates the topic of the page.
- ◆ **Text content**: General verbiage that describes, explains, and informs.
- ◆ **Graphical content**: Images that support and illustrate the text content or background images that enhance the message of the page.
- ◆ **Multimedia and interactive content**: Customized web interface features and applications that may include audio or video content to involve users in useful interaction with the site.

You must design the elements listed within the framework that define the universe of your site. The framework usually consists of:

- ◆ **A layout system or grid** that organizes the elements of a page within a given section.
- ◆ **Color palettes** that define the general color scheme of your site—graphics, text, links, background colors.
- ◆ **A font system**, otherwise known as a style sheet, that standardizes different font styles, typefaces, and sizes for different uses, such as headers and regular copy.

Specific parts of this framework are discussed in greater detail in the following sections.

MOTOROLA ANNUAL REPORT: FROM PRINT TO PIXELS

By law, the content of a web site adaptation of an annual report cannot differ in any way from the print version. Any differences, aesthetic or compositional, need to be subtle. The variations cannot alter the general presentation of info and add subjective differences. An online annual report needs to be as consistent with the print version as possible. You are repurposing materials— doing exactly what you're not supposed to do in web design. You are flat out repurposing a printed medium for the web.

As with the online version of the Motorola Annual Report that we have done two years in a row, certain things need to be changed to make it fit the medium. First, instead of it making a linear piece, you need to make a cross-navigable presentation so that people can jump from one section to another. You are no longer looking at information page by page; you are absorbing it section by section. When some people adapt print materials for the web, they assume that you have to abandon much of the original look and feel of the piece because you are working within the limitations of the web. At Adjacency, we refuse to accept this. The Motorola annual report featured several spreads with large photos in a decidedly horizontal format. Because a primary goal of the project was to ensure that all the pages would be viewable within a 640×480 window, we couldn't translate these horizontal formats without scaling the photos down dramatically, which weakens their impact. Our solution was to rearrange the layouts in a vertical format, thereby maintaining the original designer's vision.

Another important consideration in adapting printed content for the web is understanding how people interact with the information on different mediums. When you design for print, you design something that people interact with from left to right. Elements are divided by pages and spreads, whereas online information moves from top to bottom. Therefore, tables on a web page must be oriented vertically instead of horizontally. We took the Motorola At A Glance spread and reversed the categories and headings to enable web users to view the information from top to bottom instead having them scroll horizontally in order to view the information exactly as it is on the printed annual report.

Annual reports, especially if the company did well that year, have huge full-bleed images because there are no bandwidth limitations on print. Even though we have the technology to shrink image file sizes, we include huge mood shots. We realize that the web audience for an annual report includes accountants, investors, and analysts who are there for the numbers, not the pictures. Graphics were toned and scaled down the to keep the focus on the financial figures while maintaining the mood or spirit of the original piece. The people who view an annual report don't do it because it's cool. They want information, and they want it fast.

Because we assume that an audience for online annual reports usually has slower connections and more basic browsers, we go so far as to create light, scaled-down versions of the sites for people who can't even view tables. We automatically assume that the user is going to be less technologically proficient than the usual web surfer, so everything is bumped down technologically. Therefore, annual reports are not a place for advanced technologies or any heavy-bandwidth content that prohibits people from getting to your site quickly, such as Java, JavaScript, or Shockwave.

Formatting an annual report is another crucial concern. You need to line up the financials perfectly! The Motorola annual report included some particularly complex financial tables. Creating these pages in Quark would have been a daunting prospect, and yet we had to create them in HTML! With great attention to detail and a few hours of table-wrangling, we produced a web page that could easily have been mistaken for its printed counterpart.

It also makes a lot of sense to have downloadable PDF versions of the annual report. Most accountants and shareholders want to keep the annual report information for their records. Be aware that you need to look out occasionally for glitchy formatting between different versions of Adobe Acrobat Reader. We test on 2.0 through the current version, as well as on different platforms.

Because of the major legal and accounting implications, you need to check the annual report on every platform, browser, and window size. You need to throw 100% of your resources towards testing. Right after electronic commerce, annual reports are the most serious forms of web content.

Although adapting print materials for the web may seem simple and straightforward, several issues affect your layout and presentation. As with any project, we try to make sure that the information is organized well and expressed clearly.

SET UP A LAYOUT SYSTEM

Because you can never be absolutely sure of your users' platform, browser, and browser window size, you must design an interface within a grid that accommodates any kind of page and any elements. Your layout system must provide a consistent look and feel between different section areas. When you standardize the layouts for your pages, you create a continuous and seamless presentation that clearly presents the site content. A consistent layout grid enables users to focus on the content without being distracted by an incongruous, inconsistent page.

Your layout system must be expandable and collapsible. A flexible layout makes your design modular and simplifies your production process. You won't have to reinvent your page layout every time you have new content that is too big or too small for your original grid. In addition, you can accommodate various browser window sizes when you design an expandable and collapsible page. Everything should fit proportionally within a page no matter how wide or narrow (within reason) someone resizes their window. The Land Rover vehicle page demonstrates this principle (see Figure 3.13). At regular size, the elements on the page look fine. When the window is expanded out to fit within a wider screen, the layout still looks tight. Elements don't appear to be floating in a sea of accidental empty space.

Figure 3.13

When designing a web page you must take into account everyone from the low-end, workstation-challenged user to the 21-inch screen, high end graphics card power user. As with the majority of Adjacency's sites, LandRover.com was designed to accomodate varied browser window and monitor sizes through expandable/collapsable page structure and by moving essential navigation as high and to the left as possible.

The majority of web users view web pages in a 640×480-pixel screen. Although some web audiences may have larger monitors and higher resolution capabilities, designing for the 640×480 accommodates the largest common denominator of user experiences. If you design a page beyond these boundaries, you force the 640×480 people to scroll both horizontally and vertically, diminishing the impact of the page's message. Keep in mind that the window space for your web page content depends on the user's browser and the amount and type of browser buttons visible. In other words, you actually have less than 640×480 pixels to work with. On a Macintosh, for example, using Netscape Navigator with all of the maximum size buttons and location field visible gives you a surface area of only 625×325 pixels. Even if your page must scroll vertically, you need to fit the page's critical information at the top within this limited space (see Figure 3.14).

Figure 3.14

Even intentionally unconventional web page layouts such as LandRover.com's Vehicles section menu page should try to accomodate screens as small as 640×480 pixels.

DIFFERENTIATE BETWEEN PRIMARY AND SECONDARY

No matter how large or small your web site is, you must package your information in a well-organized manner. People need to be able to walk through your site and focus on the information they need while being aware of the available options. The information they need lies within a

specific subsection of your site, whereas the main menu links represent all the available options. Dividing your site into main sections and subsections enables users to absorb the content in digestible chunks.

Consider the fact that several users may enter your site through a third-tier, subsection page rather than the home page. A search engine site perhaps may lead visitors to a URL many layers down into your site. Such visitors don't experience the benefits of walking through the main doorway of your site that most clearly and obviously indicates what site it is. They need to know where they are, what information or message is on the page, and where everything else is (see Figure 3.15).

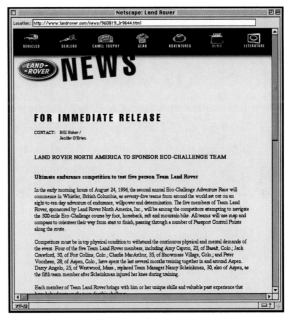

Figure 3.15

In so messy a medium as the web, site visitors should never be uncertain as to whether they're within your site or not. Even less glamourous, content-heavy pages—especially those pages—such as the LandRover.com News section press release pages, should be prominently and consistently branded.

SET UP A CLEAR NAVIGATIONAL SYSTEM

Now that you've narrowed down the sections of the site, you need to create a navigational system that's as unobtrusive as possible to free up space for design and content elements. Minimalism is your goal. We advise no more than five to ten main section links. Options are good, but too many options overwhelm and confuse users, not to mention distract them from what's truly important on the page. Starting with the basics, you can create a visual system for hypertext links and move on to more graphical navigational elements.

Links used to be easy. When they were hypertext, they underlined themselves. The underline distinguished the word from the other words on the page—the plain old unlinked words. And if the underline didn't do the trick, the link and visited link color—if done right, a different color than the other text on the page—would help visitors spot the "hot" words. But that was then.

Then designers such as Adjacency decided hypertext wasn't pretty and they wanted to further visually differentiate between content and navigation with neat, often stylized, type. Designers began to make decisions that browser-interpreted HTML used to dictate.

As with many other aspects of effective web site design, interface design is usually furthered by consistency. Consistent font selection, consistent image processing and stylization, consistent navigational element placement, and consistent link

hierarchy are all necessary when creating navigational schemes. Consistent interface design from page to page makes for intuitive, easy use. Every time a visitor hits a web site for the first time, he or she must, in essence, learn how to navigate the web all over again. Except for a few very limited instances, the better the interface design—the more consistent, the more self-evident—the quicker the visitor is able to discover how to find the information he or she's after (see Figures 3.16 and 3.17).

Figure 3.16

Each section of the PowerBar site has a primary color and a secondary color. The primary color is used to highlight the current section in the navigation frame, whereas the secondary color highlights the section the user is about to click. Descriptive text in the status bar of the window gives the user additional information about the section they are about to visit.

Figure 3.17

The side menus in the PowerBar site use a typeface called Bob's Left Hand for a loose, casual look. When the user points at a link, an underline appears, reminiscent of traditional hyperlinks but with a sketched appearance in accordance with the look and feel of the typeface.

USING CLIENT-SIDE IMAGEMAPS

Occasionally, using one large image on a page representing a group of buttons or some other set of objects makes sense. You may, however, still want to have the objects take users to different pages when clicked. This problem was solved quite some time ago, using something called a server-side imagemap. This technique consists of mapping out different regions of an image and associating a URL with each region. This list of regions (usually defined as circles, polygons, or rectangles) is called an imagemap. When the user clicks the image, the browser, sends the x-y coordinates (from the top left corner of the image) of the location the user clicked to the server, which determines if the click location falls within any of the predefined regions. If so, the user is redirected to the URL associated with that region (see Figure 3.18).

This solution is perfect except for three small drawbacks. First, when pointing at the image, the browser usually displays only the x-y coordinates in its status bar. Many users are accustomed to gaining some info about a link they might follow by looking at the URL before clicking. Server-side imagemaps do not enable this luxury.

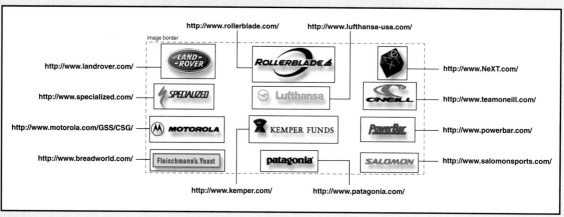

Figure 3.18

When the user clicks an imagemap, the location of their click is sent to the server as X and Y coordinates. If those coordinates fall within any of the imagemap's predefined regions, the browser is redirected to the URL associated with that region.

The second drawback is that while the server is determining if the click location falls in one of the predefined regions, the user is forced to wait. The processing required to determine where to send the user adds an additional delay to an already sluggish medium.

The third problem is that sites relying on server-side imagemaps for navigation are unusable offline, such as when viewing a site stored on a local disk.

Recognizing these drawbacks, some folks set out to create a new way of mapping images. The solution that was developed is known as a client-side imagemap. The fundamental differences are reflected in the difference in the name. Where the imagemap and location processing was previously done by the server, this information is now handled by the client, also known as the browser. This simple change solved all three of the main problems associated with server-side imagemaps. Because the browser processes the map, it knows the URL associated with a region and can display it immediately in the status bar. By the same token, the browser knows immediately where to send users when they click. And as there is no dependence on a server, the site can be moved to a local drive and maintain all of its functionality.

The syntax for creating client-side imagemaps is pretty simple. A typical map looks something like this:

```
<MAP NAME="navbar_map">
<AREA    SHAPE=RECT    COORDS="0,0,100,20"
HREF="/index.html">
<AREA    SHAPE=RECT    COORDS="101,0,200,20"
HREF="/news/news.html">
<AREA    SHAPE=RECT    COORDS="201,0,300,20"
HREF="/money/money.html">
<AREA    SHAPE=RECT    COORDS="301,0,400,20"
HREF="/life/life.html">
</MAP>
```

Note the opening and closing <MAP> tags. Between them, you place an <AREA> tag for each region of the image you wish to define. Each <AREA> tag describes the shape of the region, the coordinates defining that shape, and the associated URL. Valid shapes also include CIRC, for circle, and POLY, for polygon.

The imagemap is typically placed at the beginning of the document, after the opening <BODY> tag. To associate the map with a particular image, add the USEMAP attribute to the image, followed by a pound sign and the name of the map. For example:

```
<IMG   SRC="images/navbar.gif"   BORDER=0
USEMAP="#navbar_map">
```

Fortunately, most of the browsers in use today are capable of parsing client-side imagemaps. For those few that don't, you can provide an alternative means of navigation in two different ways. One way is to link the image to an old-style server-side imagemap as well as the client-side map by adding an ISMAP attribute alongside the USEMAP attribute. Newer browsers that are capable of using client-side imagemaps ignore the ISMAP attribute; older browsers similarly ignore the USEMAP attribute.

The second alternative is an old standby: the proverbial text links at the bottom of the page. Believe it or not, there are still quite a few people using text-only browsers. If you are kind enough to provide such an alternative, your users will thank you.

The recommendations in this section are based on the assumption that you plan to create a navigational system that goes beyond using simple, straight HTML text. We assume that you want to create a main menu that utilizes graphics, whether you plan on using static images, animation, or rollovers. Whatever the case, your navigation should be legible and integrated with the entire page—the typography and other stylistic elements. Most importantly, you must make sure that the main section links stand out enough to be read as navigational elements. Your navigation needs to look functional. It needs to look clickable! Use bevels, dropshadows, or backlighting to create a slightly three-dimensional look for your navigational graphics (See Figure 3.19). You need to add such effects to your graphics to distinguish them from the two-dimensional images and text that make up the regular content of the page. In Chapter 4 we discuss how to use interactivity to enhance your graphical navigational elements by using rollovers.

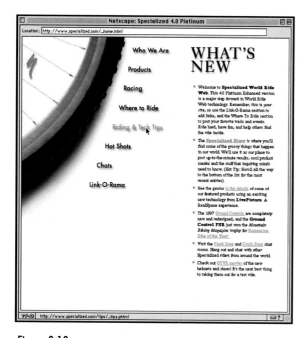

Figure 3.19

Adjacency's latest reincarnation of the Specialized World Ride Web site continues the tradition of using 3D, drop shadowed words as the basis of the navigational array.

To some extent, web browsers help make certain items clickable. When you roll over something "hot," whether it is a linked graphic or hypertext link, the cursor changes from an arrow to a pointing hand. Users might also notice that a destination URL appears in the lower left-hand status bar when they roll over a link. When they roll over an imagemapped graphic, however, they see a cryptic URL with the changing coordinates of the mouse as it moves over the graphic. Therefore, we have included a sidebar in this section that details how to create a client-side imagemap that enables users to see the true destination URL instead of the mouse's x-y coordinates.

When you design your navigational system, you must accommodate the primary and secondary links. Most of Adjacency designs employ a horizontal main section array that remains on the page throughout the site. A vertical navigational bar is added for secondary links. We find that working top down reinforces the site structure in a subtle

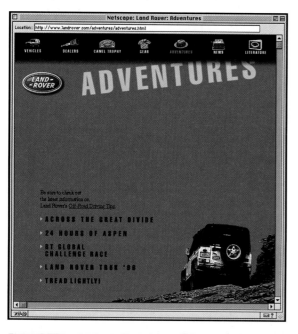

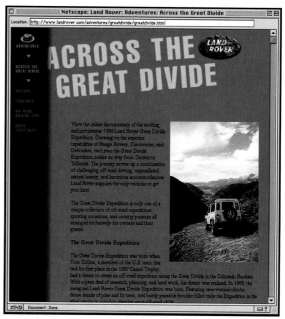

Figure 3.20

On LandRover.com, Adjacency designed two varieties of menu bars to serve different purposes. The site and section menu pages feature icons running across the top of the page that link to the main areas of the site. Subsection pages feature left-side, vertically running hierarchical section and page name links that reveal section structure.

way that is almost reminiscent of menu bars and pull-down or drop-down menus that most operating systems use. Using different layout devices to distinguish between your main and subsection links helps users know where to find links to the information they need (See Figure 3.20). If you change where and how you place the navigation at any step of the way, you disorient users. They won't know what to expect. Above all else, your navigational elements must stand out in constant, predictable places.

Emphasizing and de-emphasizing the navigation deliberately for different pages hints to users how deep they are within the site. The closer you are to the top level of the site, the more graphical and prominent the navigation appears. It may take up more real estate and may use more colors or even brighter, bolder colors compared with sublevel pages. These upper-level pages can afford to have more prominent navigational elements because they tend to have less content on them. The idea is to get users to click, to move down within your site and between different sections. You want your audience to explore your site. The content on these main pages summarizes what lies within the section so that users can see at a glance where they might go and what they might find.

When you go further down into a site, the navigational elements tend to exist as an aside. The focus of the page becomes the actual content (see Figure 3.21). The navigation may look the same but more subdued. What stands out now is the current section highlighted within the navigation. This one accent lets users know where they are in the site and de-emphasizes the entire navigational bar or element as a whole so that users can absorb the main content of the page.

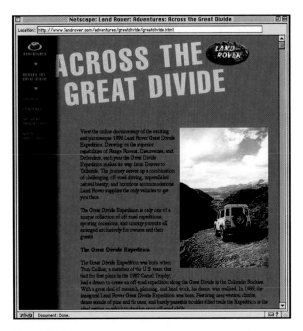

Figure 3.21

The deeper you progress into a site, Adjacency tends to design pages less for funneling visitors to areas elswhere in the site and more for presenting information. A good navigation system design is highly apparent on sparsely populated pages without competing loudly for attention with the information on content-rich pages.

With JavaScript, you can create an unobtrusive navigational system, such as vertical nested navigational items, and therefore minimize the navigational scheme. Only one item shows when inactive, but it expands when activated by a rollover or click. These types of techniques free up the page for more content layout. As we mentioned before, Chapter 4 discusses these techniques in greater detail. We like to mention rollovers in navigational systems to open up your mind to different design possibilities.

These fancy features may not be so intuitive, however. Eventually more and more people will learn and web standards will change the same way design standards change. Until then, your navigational system, and general layout, for that matter, must be intuitive and obvious. Without setting up clear navigational links, you defeat the purpose of navigation on your site. The next chapter, which discusses interactivity, offers specific suggestions and techniques, such as rollovers, on how to enhance your navigation to engage users.

One final but important element your navigational system should include is a way back to the main menu or home page. It's our job to let people know where they are and where they're going. We also want to let them step back and start over. It's an unavoidable fact of life that people want the chance to start at the beginning of your site. We usually provide a hot link back to the main menu through the site's company logo (see Figure 3.22).

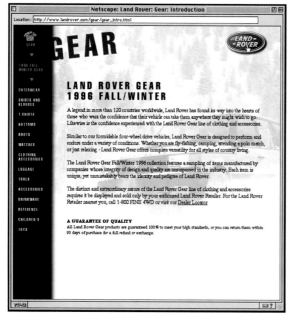

Figure 3.22

Adjacency tends to place a client's logo consistently on every page of a site for branding and as a return link to the starting point of a site. Clicking Land Rover's logo, for instance, sends visitors to the site's main menu page.

USE DIFFERENT BUT COMPLEMENTARY LOOKS FOR EACH SECTION

Different levels should have different looks but still fit together and still look related to each other and to the general look and feel of the site. Color is the easiest way to differentiate between sections as well as to get extra boom on a page. Color is free! You don't need fancy graphics that take up lots of kilobytes. When you first start designing a site, you can work simply with color. High-level pages deserve high-level impact. Use color in combination with "empty" space. Color a design element that leads your users' eyes to the information they need. Take advantage of HTML <BODY> background colors. Unless you create a gradient or combination of different, complicated tones, you're getting impact at no cost to you. Use color to accent the current section in the navigation as in the example above. Use color for large and small areas, and don't be afraid to experiment. Remember to stick to your color palette that ties your site together. In the end, use color sparingly. You need a good reason for anything you do (see Figure 3.23).

Using graphics is the next obvious way to differentiate between sites. Section logos or icons coupled with the section title help brand each individual section, while the company logo in a consistent spot on each page ties them all together. The different graphics for the different sections obviously illustrate different ideas and information, but be sure that they use a consistent style, share a common color palette, and conform to the layout system or grid you established (see Figure 3.24).

Figure 3.23

As with many well-designed web sites, PowerBar.com and the original Salomon hiking site derive strong visual unity from the varied combinations of colors from their own consistent site color palette.

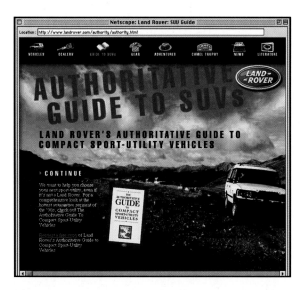

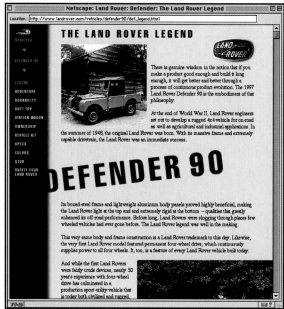

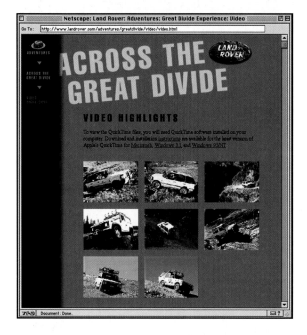

Figure 3.24

Careful and deliberate variation among logos can be used to brand different sections within a site. A great example of a site that uses this strategy effectively is Land Rover. Several sections sport differentiated Land Rover badges: the majority of the sections feature the jeweled Land Rover oval badge while the area of the site that describes the history of the marque displays a vintage badge in the place of the contemporary and off-road driving-related pages wear a muddied version of the modern oval.

In general, different graphic implementations on a web page include:

◆ Small background strips or repeating tiles

◆ Large background images using photographs or illustrations

◆ Images with small file sizes embedded on the page to support the text content

◆ Images with larger file sizes embedded on the page to support the text content or in fact, serve as the actual content and focus of the page

CREATING BACKGROUND JPEGS

One of the best means of integrating type and photography is to throw your image onto the background of the page and lay your text over it using transparent GIFs and hypertext (see Figure 3.25). For this to work effectively, your background image should be at least 640×480 pixels (the typical minimum browser window size) and as large as 1,024×768 pixels, the size available on some of the larger displays.

Figure 3.25

The background image from a recent Rollerblade.com site menu is designed to fit within a 640×480pixel area, while offering visitors with larger monitors even more bang for their bandwidth.

Unfortunately, background images large enough to fill a browser window can easily be over 100K or more in size if you're not careful. On a typical modem connection, this translates into roughly 100–200 seconds of waiting on the part of end users. Don't count on them to be so patient.

Measures can be taken to reduce the size of your background JPEGs. The simplest way is to reduce the physical dimensions of the image. This, of course, increases the likelihood that your image may not fill the user's window; you decide if this is acceptable or not depending on the design goals of your page.

Even at greater dimensions, there is always the possibility that the user's window is larger than your image. You can prepare for this possibility by ensuring that there is a smooth transition between tiles. This can in some cases call for some extensive photo-manipulation, but if done well, this technique can actually further the success of your design (see Figure 3.26).

Figure 3.26

The background for the Land Rover site menu is designed to fill the typical browser window without tiling. It is, however, padded with black (roughly the same width as the navigation bar) to provide a transition between tiles in the event that the site visitor is using a larger window.

Another way to buy yourself some real estate is to increase the compression applied to parts of your image that are less important than others. Because the bottom and right sides of the image are more likely to be cropped by the window, for example, you can sacrifice more image quality there than you might want to in the rest of your image. This selective compression is done by blurring the area you wish to compress more than the rest. Using a graphics tool such as Photoshop, select the desired area, preferably with a feathered selection, and apply a Gaussian Blur of 0.3 to 2.0 pixels in radius. Because the blur reduces contrast in the selected area, that part of your image is more conducive to greater JPEG compression.

You need to determine the most bandwidth-efficient option or combination of options. If you can still achieve 80 percent of the original impact of your design by using less-detailed, flatter images, then the compromise is worth it. You still deliver high impact and, this time around, a faster impact. The next section discusses the compromises you have to make in preparing graphics for the web in order for your user to have the most enjoyable experience possible. Although the next section discusses the different issues and considerations for using certain graphics file formats, two sidebars here help you achieve a distinctive look and feel for your section pages. They involve using big, bold photographic images and creating a full bleed effect on a web page.

MAKING IMAGES BLEED OFF THE PAGE

One of the most dramatic differences between print design and web design is the ability to create relationships between the elements of the page and the edge of the page. Making images bleed off the edge of the page is quite common in designing print materials to creating a striking visual that reinforces the overall unity of the design by tying page elements to the material on which they are printed.

When Adjacency was founded, conventional wisdom held that this couldn't be done on a web page because the edge of the "page" could be anywhere on the user's screen depending on how large their browser window was. Adjacency refused to accept this and set out to prove that those who listen to conventional wisdom are fools.

At the time, tables were just coming into widespread use on the Internet. Site designers such as Adjacency loved them; they enabled us to more closely replicate the layout controls we had been brought up using in the world of print design. In perusing the white papers on how tables worked on Netscape's site, we noticed that you could specify table width as a percentage of the window width, in values of 0 to 100. But what would happen if you specified a table width of 110%? We tried it, and sure enough, the contents of the table ran just beyond the right edge of the window. But unfortunately, this large table also introduced an ugly scrollbar at the bottom of the screen. If the user clicked the scrollbar, the image we were trying to bleed would scroll completely into view.

To get around this, we created a table with a width of 100%, and then placed a second table with a width of 110% within the first table. See Figure 3.27 for an illustration of how this looks. Obviously, a larger table shouldn't be able to fit inside a smaller one, but due to a bug in Netscape's table parsing, this anomaly was ignored. The browser seemed to assume that the contents of the page were set to 100%, not 110%, so the window's scrollbars no longer showed up. Voilà! A full-page bleed. No matter how large or small the user's window was, no matter if they resized it and resized it again, the image would always bleed just off the right-hand side of the page.

Figure 3.27

With table borders turned on, you can see how the first table is set to a width of 100%. The first row of this table contains the navigation bar, Land Rover logo, and page head. The second row contains a table with a width of 110%, causing the image to bleed off the right-hand side of the page.

We were quite proud of our ability to turn Netscape's bug into a feature, but unfortunately, the browser company has decided to fix this bug in the newest release of Navigator, so this trick's days are numbered.

There is another way to pull this off using frames. Although originally scorned by many site designers for their ugly borders and buggy implementation, frames are fast becoming a choice technology, especially in light of some changes made in the newer versions of Navigator and Internet Explorer. Both now enable you to use borderless frames and to position elements exactly along the edge of the window by specifying the margin width and margin height of a frame. (Almost. Netscape actually doesn't recognize margin widths or margin heights less than 1, so you always have one pixel of background color showing along the edge of your frames. See Accommodating the Multitude of Browsers and Platforms, earlier in this chapter, for more information on this.)

If you build a site using borderless frames, you can give the impression of full-bleed images by making your images align left or right, bypassing the confusion of tables altogether. An additional advantage to this method is that it enables you to bleed images on all sides of the page, whereas the table trick was limited to bleeding images to the right and bottom. Finally, this method works reliably across browsers and platforms, giving it another advantage over using tables.

SCRUNCHING IMAGES: WAIT VS. REWARD

Give as much boom per kilobyte as possible—our goal with every client. With each image, we ask ourselves, "Is this a cool and compelling enough image? Is there something else on the page that will load while this loads? Is it worth the wait?" Too many sites make you sit and wait for heavy and oversized graphics that don't add value to the content of the page. If you're going to make your users wait, the final result should wow them, should blow them away! This section helps you take advantage of HTML and different manipulation techniques to deliver web graphics with as much "POW" and speed as possible.

USE HTML TO HELP YOU

Some basic HTML code can help you create a perception of a faster download time. On the Adjacency home page, we use an `<IMG LOWSRC>` technique that loads a light GIF before the heavier and detailed JPEG navigational menu (see Figure 3.28). We wanted to be able to present our clients' logos boldly and prominently, but we also wanted to address our users who would be too impatient to wait for the final image to load. The low source image enables such visitors to see the available links right away and click to the desired destination.

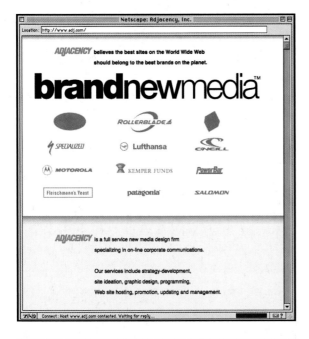

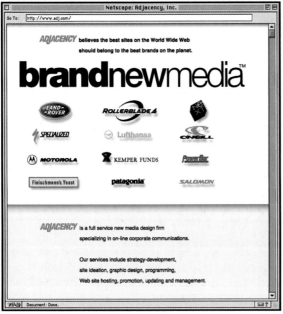

Figure 3.28

The Adjacency home page uses `<IMG LOWSRC>` *to enable impatient users to click desired destinations right away, while leaving a stunning JPEG for those who prefer to wait just a little bit longer.*

You can also manually set the widths and heights of your images to load the other nongraphical content first while the images are downloading. By adding `WIDTH=` and `HEIGHT=` to your `<IMG SRC>` tag, you are helping the browser know what to expect. It won't have to go all the way to the server right away to get all of the graphics information before downloading the other elements of the page. If you already have an entire site with images that don't have specified dimensions in the HTML, you can run a script to insert them automatically. We encourage you to check out our companion web site at `http://www.adj.com/killer/` for more information and details on this script.

When you decide to visually enhance your pages with graphics, ask yourself if you truly need to use a graphic. Now that you can specify typefaces in your HTML, you can create distinctive typography on your content pages instead of using graphics simply by using `FACE` in your `<FONT>` tag. You can also provide alternatives for Mac and Windows users by separating the different font choices with a comma:

```
<FONT FACE="Helvetica, Arial">text</FONT>.
```

See Figure 3.2 for an example of how this can benefit a page design.

When specifying fonts, we recommend using only standard system font typefaces (see Figure 3.29). Specifying a font that only you and ten other people have on their hard drives won't do you much good. If someone who doesn't have the specified font visits your site, he or she won't be able to benefit from your intended effect.

Figure 3.29

System fonts for both Mac and Windows machines.

REBUFFING THE SMALL GRAPHICS/SMALL PAGE MYTH

The prevailing school of thought regarding fast page loads has always held that images need to be small in dimension in order for them to be acceptably small in file size. This is simply not true.

The accompanying figures show pages that contradict this widely held belief. The Land Rover Discovery page, for example (Figure 3.30), uses a background that is 915×700 pixels high, enough to fill almost any browser window. The file size for the image is only 22K, however. Similarly, the background for the Skate Parks page (Figure 3.31) is 700×550 pixels but under 10K in file size.

Figure 3.30

Land Rover's Discovery vehicle section intro page background image is 915×700 pixels, yet remarkably only 22k.

Figure 3.31

This 700×550 pixel background from the Rollerblade site is under 10k in file size.

You can also give a page a "large feel" by using big background type. The PowerGel page shown in Figure 3.32, for example, uses a full-screen background GIF that contains the PowerGel catch phrase "Rip it and surge!" This background is 700×900 pixels but only 9K in size.

Once you learn that images don't have to be small in dimension in order to download quickly, you open a whole new set of possibilities. You should take this opportunity to rethink web design in terms of the whole page. Don't restrict yourself to linear thinking, building pages that start with a header GIF that is followed by some text that is followed by an image that is followed by some more text. Seek to create an integrated whole in which every part of the page relates to the others.

The Kemper site menu, for example (see Figure 3.33), employs a design in which every element relates to all the others, largely through the unifying scheme of the circle. The Lufthansa-USA site menu (see Figure 3.34) achieves its integrated design by drawing on the look and feel of much of Lufthansa's print collateral. By building the page as a whole, you can present your user with a more cohesive page, with more clearly stated choices

presented to them. Users are more likely to return to a site—and to recommend it to others—if they are rewarded for their trouble with an innovative visual experience.

Figure 3.32

PowerBar.com's PowerGel web page features a 700×900 pixel GIF background that's only 9K in file size.

Figure 3.33

The Kemper site menu employs a circular scheme that unifies its elements, all centered around the Kemper.com masthead that rests solidly on the horizontal line created by the background image. The overall effect is that of a larger image, but the layout is really an assemblage of several smaller, precisely aligned pieces.

Figure 3.34

The Lufthansa-USA.com site menu integrates a medium-sized image of the view from a window seat into a black background. By making the transition from image to background seamless, the page assumes a more unified, poster-like effect.

THERE'S A NEW KID IN TOWN: PNG

Although the vast majority of images on the web are in either of the GIF or JPEG formats, a new format has appeared on the horizon. It's name is PNG, short for Portable Network Graphics and pronounced "ping." PNG holds a lot of promise for web developers.

Designed to replace the older and simpler GIF format, PNG is a lossless compression format with a slew of new features that make GIF look like yesterday's potatoes. These features include:

◆ Truecolor support: Whereas GIF images are restricted to a palette of 256 colors or less, PNG enables for full 24-bit color RGB images. It also supports grayscale and palette images.

◆ Alpha channels: Whereas GIF only enables you to specify a single color from your image as transparent, PNG enables you to specify transparency as an alpha channel. This is a grayscale image that specifies the transparency of each pixel in your image using varying shades of gray. You could, for example, use an opaque oval with blurred edges as your alpha channel, and the image area within that oval would appear antialiased against any background you put it on. The same image could be used in multiple places without the ugly ghosting that appears around GIF images.

◆ Gamma correction: You may have noticed that images created on a Macintosh often appear too dark on a PC, and that PC images appear to light on a Mac. Using gamma correction, a PNG image is able to account for the varying brightness from monitor to monitor. Although the manner in which this works is beyond the scope of this book, suffice it to say that built-in gamma correction enables more consistent display from platform to platform and from screen to screen.

◆ Two-dimensional interlacing: GIF uses a one-dimensional interlacing method that consists of four "passes." This interlacing is designed to give the user an idea of what the image is before all of it has downloaded. With each pass, more of the image is defined and the content becomes easier to comprehend. Because there are only 4 passes, 25 percent of the data must be received before the user gets a general overview. PNG's two-dimensional interlacing uses seven passes, with only $1/64$ of the data being transmitted in the first pass. This means the user gets an overview of the image 8-16 times faster than with GIF.

◆ Better compression: PNG is generally capable of compressing 10-30 percent better than GIF. Although it does not approach JPEG-level compression, bear in mind that PNG is a lossless compression, meaning that all of your original image data is retained. This is not the case with JPEG.

◆ Patent-free: GIF uses compression technology that belongs to Unisys, so developers who wish to create software that generates GIFs have to pay royalties on the technology. PNG uses public domain compression technology and is patent- and royalty-free.

Although PNG's advantages over GIF are many, one thing GIF does that PNG does not is animation. A multiple-image variant know as MPNG, however, is under development.

So if PNG is so great, why aren't more web developers using it? Unfortunately, the most popular web browsers, Netscape Navigator and Internet Explorer, don't support PNG natively. You can view PNG images using plug-ins, but this means using an <EMBED> tag rather than an <IMG> tag and also tends to exclude users who don't have the necessary plug-in. The rumor is that the 4.0 releases of both these browsers will support PNG natively, so keep your fingers crossed.

KEEP YOUR FILE SIZES DOWN

Keeping your file sizes down makes download times faster and potentially more rewarding. Right off the bat, knowing when to use the appropriate format for your graphics saves you. Entire books have been written on techniques for preparing web graphics and the differences between GIFs and JPEGs. We have included a visual survey of the end results of using different file formats for the same graphic (See Figure 3.35). The crucial basics are listed here:

◆ **Use JPEGs for** photographs and detailed images with extensive gradients and color variations.

◆ **Minimize JPEG file sizes by** using as many large areas of black or white as possible.

◆ **Use GIFs for** everything else—smaller icons and graphics.

◆ **Minimize GIF file sizes by** (a) making black or white transparent when you index the image. No matter how low you index a graphic, it always contains black and white. By making one of those colors transparent, you are effectively knocking out one of those colors. We have been able to make some of our images 5K smaller using this technique. (b) using the CRLI technique to add 1-pixel horizontal black or white lines that take advantage of how GIF compression works better with horizontal bands of color. See the sidebar for more details. (c) not interlacing. Interlacing adds a couple of extra kilobytes to an image.

Figure 3.35

Image 1: the original image, a PICT file
File size: 875k

Image 2: saved as a GIF, indexed at 5-bit,
Adaptive Palette, with Diffusion.
File size: 118k

Image 3: saved as a JPEG, saved at level 25.
File size: 45k

COMPRESSING GIFS WITH THE CRLI TECHNIQUE

Although JPEG is often the best compression method for squeezing really big images into really small files, there are times when the GIF compression is more suited to the task. GIF is particularly useful for compressing large areas of flat color, especially when dealing with images that have rows of flat color.

You can take advantage of this by using a technique called CRLI ("curly"), which is a means of preparing your images so that they are more compressible when you save them as GIFs. CRLI stands for Consecutive Run-Length Insertion, but all you need to remember is that you replace every other row of your image with a solid color to create a more compressible image.

The background GIF for the PowerBar Nutrition Guide page is an example (Figure 3.36). By using the CRLI technique, we were able to compress an image that is 700×1,000 pixels in size down to only 14K. The same image, without the CLRI technique applied, was 36K. Saving the image as a medium-quality Photoshop JPEG yielded a 26K file, complete with all of the blotchy artifacts typical of JPEG files.

CRLI creates a more highly compressible file because of GIF's proficiency at compressing horizontal regions of the same color. Examine the magnification shown in Figure 3.36 for a closer look at how CRLI works.

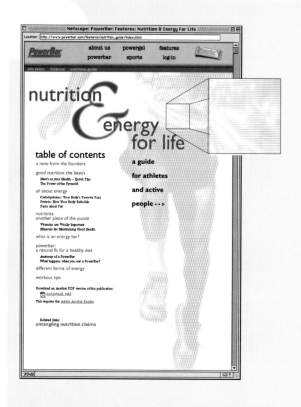

Figure 3.36

The PowerBar Nutrition Guide features PowerBar founder Brian Maxwell running in the background. Note how CRLI is used to reduce the file size.

No matter what image editor you prefer, implementing the CRLI technique is fairly straightforward. If you use Adobe Photoshop, you can follow these steps:

1. Open the image you wish to compress using CRLI.

2. Create a new image, 1 pixel wide, 2 pixels high, with a transparent background.

3. Using the Pencil tool, fill one of the pixels with the color you want to use for every other row in your final image.

4. Select all and choose Define Pattern from the Edit menu.

5. Close this 2-pixel image. (You may want to save it for future use.)

6. In your original image, create a new layer above those you want to affect. Name the layer CRLI.

7. Choose Fill from the Edit menu and fill the layer with the Pattern you just created.

8. Duplicate your image, flatten its layers, index, and save as a GIF.

Because CRLI calls for replacing half your image with a solid color, it tends to reduce the contrast dramatically. Although photorealistic content doesn't lend itself to CRLI compression, it can be perfect for illustrative images that you want to use a backdrop for the rest of your page.

In general, you can compress your images by using a limited color palette and as few colors as possible. More colors equal more K, and the larger areas of color, the better.

Remember that you always have to compromise when preparing your web graphics and designing the entire interface. The entire look and feel of the site must strike a balance between clarity and graphical impact. You achieve clarity by designing an intuitive navigational system for a well-organized site. Graphical impact happens through the colors you choose, the layout you design, and the graphics you create. These combined elements should communicate a specific message and project a distinctive identity or character. Designing an interface is no small task! But with some practice, perseverance, and constant communication with your client, you will approach and achieve better web designs.

TEST, TEST, TEST

Designing a web site doesn't end with the completion of a final product. It's an ongoing process that cycles through different phases of designing, testing, and redesigning. We recommend that you review the sidebar in Chapter 2, "Accommodating the Multitude of Browsers and Platforms," and study the figures included to understand the differences in the appearance on the various browsers and platforms. Here is a checklist of things that we test with and look out for:

♦ **Platforms**: Sites are tested on both Macintosh and Windows machines. Although we predominantly develop our sites using Macs, we know that the majority of web surfers use PCs.

♦ **Browsers**: When developing a site, we ensure that the page structures we create as the basis for the site render acceptably on all current and upcoming versions of Internet Explorer and Netscape Navigator. We also test older versions of these browsers, as the average web user doesn't always download the latest browser version the moment it becomes available. In addition, we test on many of the less popular browsers, such as Mosaic, America Online's custom browser, and Cyderdog. (Of course, we often find that these browsers just aren't up to the challenge of displaying our enhanced sites. For this reason, we encourage people using these browsers to use our lite sites.)

♦ **Varying screen and window sizes**: Not everyone has a 21-inch monitor, so we test to ensure that our pages fit in the smallest browser window, typically around 640×480, while still rendering reasonably well on large monitors. In some cases this means using fixed table widths of 600 pixels or so, whereas on other sites we allow the content to stretch to fill the whole screen, as long as it is still readable.

♦ **Color depth**: Although most of our production machines are capable of displaying thousands of colors or more, we recognize that many people are still using 256 and even 16 color systems. We preview all of our sites on low-color machines to ensure that a JPEG background looks great in both thousands of colors as well as 256 colors.

♦ **Images**: The site is checked for any broken icons. We check the ALT text when images are turned off in the browser. We make sure that images are properly transparent. (To do this, click the image and hold down the mouse to "View this image." The browser loads a new window with the image and you can verify whether or not it's transparent.)

◆ **Links**: We make sure that links work! Obviously, going through a site page by page and checking every link can be an overwhelming and time-consuming process. Fortunately, there are tools available for many platforms to help facilitate and even automate this process. See the companion site to this book for more information on these tools.

◆ **Alignment**: We generally scan for any major or basic alignment problems that jump out at us, like unclosed <CENTER> tags. If we've created a customized background, we check to make sure that text doesn't run over the border of the background image. In other words, we make sure that a background tile repeats itself in such a way that the user won't be able to tell that it does repeat itself. We also try to make sure that our forms aren't misaligned.

◆ **Title Bar**: Each page is checked to make sure it has a title and that the title bar corresponds with the page content.

◆ **Forms**: Forms are checked to ensure that it is clear to the user what they need to fill out and we test to ensure that the submission process works as expected.

◆ **Java and JavaScript**: Rollovers, customized alert boxes, pop-up windows, and other special scripts are checked to make sure that they're working. We check any applets to see if they are working properly.

◆ **CGI scripts**: Scripts are checked to make sure that they're doing their job.

◆ **Text content**: As much as possible, the copy is scanned to make sure that everything makes sense.

Again, this is a basic list of things to look out for. When in doubt, good old fashioned common sense will save you.

SUMMARY

If you want your web site to pack a punch, you must be willing to invest the time and energy to create effective page layouts and exciting graphics. When people walk away from your site, they remember the graphics, the individual page layouts, as well as the entire organization of the site. They remember how easy or difficult it was to get the information they wanted. This ease is determined by the speed, clarity, simplicity, and consistency of your pages. The aesthetic you create for your site delivers the most impact if you push the envelope on design within the context of a clearly organized interface. Users are not be satisfied with one cool graphic. They need an entire experience that engages them and opens their eyes to new information. Once you create a web site built with solid page layouts, effective navigation, and compelling, cross-platform images, you are ready to move on and incorporate enhanced interactive features.

CHAPTER
4

INTERACTIVITY IS CREATING WAYS FOR

PEOPLE TO RELATE AND CONTRIBUTE TO THE INFOR-

MATION ON A WEB SITE WITHOUT SIMPLY JUST READING A PAGE. UNLESS WE

BELIEVE THAT STATIC TEXT IS THE ULTIMATE INFORMATION DESIGN SOLUTION, IT

DESIGNING AND BUILDING interACTIVITY

STANDS

TO REA-

SON THAT

INTERACTIVITY CAN ENHANCE INFORMATION EXCHANGES.

ANYTHING THAT ENGAGES YOUR AUDIENCE AND INCITES THEM TO ACTION CAN

DEFINE INTERACTIVITY ON YOUR WEB SITE. INTERACTIVITY INVOLVES A TWO-WAY DIA-

LOG. FOR EVERY ACTION THERE IS A REACTION. USUALLY, YOU CLICK SOMEWHERE AND

SOMETHING HAPPENS, OR CONVERSELY, SOMETHING ON THE PAGE HAPPENS OR EXISTS AND

YOU CLICK SOMETHING IN RESPONSE. INTERACTIVITY ON A WEB SITE ENABLES USERS TO

INTERACT WITH THE INFORMATION, MANIPULATE THE PRESENTATION, AND CAUSE ACTIONS OR

CHANGES.

We teach you how to synthesize the concepts from the previous chapters regarding brand recognition, goals, strategies, and interface design and elevate them all to the next level. Each chapter thus far represents a critical step in developing a killer interactive web site. You cannot create a killer interactive web site without the following:

◆ Understanding your client's company and brand as discussed in Chapter 1
◆ Definitive objectives, strategies, and a planned structure as discussed in Chapter 2
◆ A solid understanding of what kinds of layouts and graphics work for the World Wide Web as discussed Chapter 3

In this chapter, we help ensure that your site enhancements are rooted in the concepts you learned in the previous chapters. Through interactivity, you are able to present your message more boldly and effectively, while gathering crucial information from user feedback and participation.

DEVELOPING INTERACTIVE FEATURES

By nature, a web site can be a thoroughly interactive medium. But you have to make it happen. You are the information architect who must make sure that your site best utilizes the nonlinear nature of the web without confusing or annoying users. You are the designer, developer, producer, programmer, marketer, or sales person. You need to come up with ideas to make content as fresh, as exciting, and as useful as possible, as well as an interface that clearly and boldly organizes that content.

This section equips you with tools to make sure you have a complete and thorough understanding of interactivity. Without this understanding, you can't use interactive features successfully on your web site. We attempt to lead you through the

plethora of web fads and technologies and help you select the most appropriate tools for your needs, your client's needs, and your audience's needs.

USE METAPHORS TO CLARIFY THE MESSAGE

Understanding the meaning of interactivity involves looking at the real world for everyday examples in order to apply understandable metaphors to a web site interface. The web still stands as a relatively new medium. Many people out there still haven't seen a web page. Others are still getting the hang of clicking hypertext links. You need to find the common denominators of experiences people have when they encounter your site.

Who will be using your web site? Most likely, people with other modern-day conveniences have Internet access. At the very basic level, people know that when they open a door or pass through a doorway, they exit one place to enter a new one. When people turn on their radios, they know and expect that music will play or people will be talking. When they turn the dial, they know they are switching stations to listen to different things. There are zillions of everyday examples where we react to or activate different mechanisms and expect certain results.

Just as we can't take a print ad and slap it onto a web page, we cannot expect all metaphors to work on the web. Metaphors carry the danger or potential for being too obvious, too cute, or too ridiculous. Metaphors help us better understand how we can make an interactive site, but they do not serve as straightforward design solutions (see Figure 4.1). We constantly have to remind ourselves that the web is its own unique medium. People understand clicking buttons as long as that's how the buttons appear. Other than that, there are still people who don't understand how to use a web browser and what to do with a web page after they get there. Unless you are using animation, people may not readily understand that they can click a static image to take them to a new page or new site.

Figure 4.1

The Saturn site does not present the user with a unified message or metaphor. Rather, each image on the page seems to assert a different metaphor than the next. The butterfly and traffic light do not link to any content; why are they there? What do they mean? The heart-car is the nearest thing to a clear metaphor, but its efficacy is diluted by the other images on the page. They fight for precedence, resulting in a mixed metaphor that leaves the user confused.

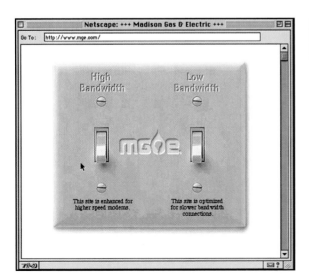
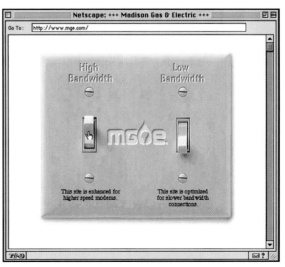

Adjacency's Madison Gas & Electric utility web site employs a clear, simple, and appropriate metaphor on its splash page: a light switch. By flipping one switch or the other, the user chooses an enhanced site or the lite site.

Never fear. People are learning. Simple things such as the cursor changing from an arrow to a pointing hand help signal to the user that they can activate something by clicking the image or text underneath this transformed cursor. Even seasoned web surfers need clear ideas of what they can do with a site and how to use it. No matter how experienced your user is, you need to make the site as intuitive as possible.

ENGAGE AND EMPOWER YOUR AUDIENCE

Throughout the book, we talk about creating useful, meaningful sites. Incorporating interactivity adds value to your web site because it engages and empowers your audience. A goal of most sites is to distribute information. Don't stop there. Give your users the ability to filter information, to see just what they want to see. Give them the ability to react to information: let them talk back and offer input on the evolution of the site. And give them the ability to add information: let them bring their own experiences to the site and share them with everyone else who visits. Allowing people to modify and participate in the flow of information gives them ownership of the site and its content in a way that most sites do not. They will thank you for it in return visits.

Although the next of half of this chapter elaborates more on implementing these personalization techniques, you should note here that successful web sites should make users feel enlightened. Using your site should be as natural and as stress-free as possible. Even a well-meaning site full of interesting information and fun tidbits can fail if it ends up confusing and overwhelming a user. When they understand that they can pick different points of destination and choose them exactly when they want, they feel like an integral part of the experience.

Information architecture should also have room for fun and entertainment. Graphical interactive features, individualized site presentations, movies, or soundtracks can also enrich a user's experience. If you add animated GIFs to your site to point people toward important parts of a page or the entire site, you help users understand the best ways to navigate through your site by highlighting items that they may not have otherwise noticed. On Lufthansa's home page we animated the "bookings" link to make it appear as though it were flying onto the page (see Figure 4.2). We added just a little bit of visual interest and drama to call attention to the link. No blinky text, no crazy colors—just a simple animation, consistent with the upward angle of the typography and airline theme, which happens after the page is downloaded.

Not only do these interactive features engage your users, but they also humanize the experience. Through interactivity, you show users that you care about who they are and what they need. You initiate a dialogue and relationship with your audience that demonstrates that you respect their time, ideas, and consideration for your company or products. Adding contact forms, threaded discussions, or chat rooms provide instruments for users to communicate with you and amongst each other. You can create an environment that relates to the real world beyond the confines of this network of computers we call the World Wide Web. This chapter contains case studies that cover personalizing your site as well as developing online communities. Sidebars are also included that discuss HTML forms, dealer locators, Java, JavaScript, and cookies.

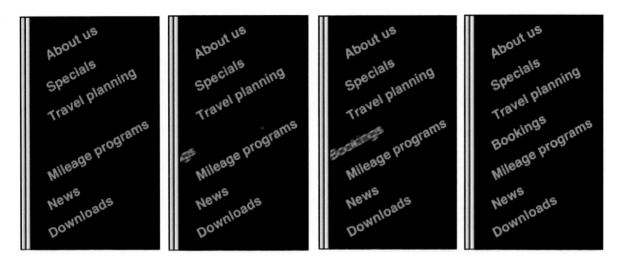

Figure 4.2

Example of an effective use of animation on Lufthansa's site.

People who visit your site either have seen it all or haven't seen enough. You need to create an experience that distinguishes your site from the millions of other sites on the web. Interactivity is the key. Interactivity adds elements of surprise and fun that help make the experience enjoyable and memorable.

DON'T USE TECHNOLOGY FOR TECHNOLOGY'S SAKE

Developing a web site starts and ends with design. Technology is simply a means to an end that serves as a tool. For the web medium to survive and be a popular broad-based medium, it has to move away from a preoccupation with the bells and whistles of the technology and move towards the end result. We wanted to avoid filling this book with a laundry list of the latest plug-ins, applications, techniques, and web browser features. Web technology moves so quickly that by the time this book gets on the shelves, there will be new versions and permutations of these tools, tips, and tricks.

Through *Creating Killer Interactive Web Sites*, we want to arm you with the instruments and skills that you can use next year, not just next month.

Why are people so preoccupied with web technology? Why are there web surfers who surf specifically to find what's latest and greatest in web technology? Because web technology changes so rapidly that people preoccupy themselves with the newness and the connection to this progress and growth. The biggest, most powerful, cash-flush companies online today are information technology companies whose business goals are directly wedded to promoting web technology. They want to promote their products. You might often find some unwarranted publicity on the technological flavor of the week. This hype and sensationalism won't disappear, but it will subside.

Technology has value because it enables us to organize information more quickly, more directly, more intuitively, and more interactively. Soon, more of our parents and next door neighbors will get online to be informed, entertained, and empowered. You cannot empower users when you overwhelm them with senseless features and poorly designed, confusing web pages. You should be able to draw from web technologies that reinforce your message and support your audience (see Figure 4.3).

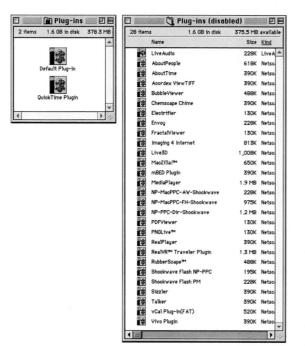

Figure 4.3

You must be selective when choosing the appropriate technologies for your site from the sea of available plug-ins. Just because you can do something, it doesn't mean you should.

To keep yourself in check, ask yourself, "Do I really need to add this to my site? Does it truly add value to the flow and presentation of my content?" Take frames, for example. The debut of frames seduced hundreds of web developers. Here was a smart, new way to organize elements on a web page to enable specific things to change, while other things could remain the same. People thought they had to use frames and reorganize their pages because it was the thing to do. Well, not all sites need frames. Frames make the most

sense for sites with several layers of information, where it would be helpful to keep main navigational links in one static frame, while content could appear in another scrollable frame.

Animated GIFs also represent a popular and somewhat overly used web technology. Yes, we are all excited about being able to make pictures move on a web page (certainly a far cry from the drab gray web pages with text-only information of yesteryear). But let's be reasonable. Two or more animations on a page are too distracting, especially when they do not relate to each other as in a page with an animated web ad banner on top of the page's animated content. Earlier, we discussed how we used an animated GIF to draw people's attention to the bookings link on the Lufthansa site. It makes its dramatic entrance, animates once, and that's it! Simple and effective. Learn how to do it yourself in this section's sidebar dedicated to creating effective animated GIFs.

In trying to figure out whether to use a particular kind of web technology, first think about the impact on your audience.

◆ If you are thinking of implementing frames, do your typical users have frames-enabled browsers?

◆ If your design calls for invisible frame borders, do your users have the appropriate version of a browser that creates this effect correctly?

◆ If your decision to use frames comes after you have already launched your site, will users be able to access pages that they have bookmarked?

◆ Are you going to force users to deal with the situation on their own, or are you going to go out of your way to create individual framesets for these pages to accommodate people who have the direct URLs?

CREATING EFFECTIVE ANIMATED GIFS

One of the most popular means of making web pages more visually appealing is adding animated GIFs. An animated GIF is a graphic that contains multiple images played in succession, and they can be quite useful for conveying a lot of information in a small space. You can, for example, use an animated GIF to create a simple slideshow, with each frame of the image displaying new information. You can bring your illustrations to life, so they not only illustrate an idea but also act it out.

These days it is difficult to find a site that doesn't contain at least one GIF animation. If used without proper forethought, however, animated GIFs can go a long way toward making your page visually displeasing—even chaotic or annoying to the eye.

This is not say that GIFs can't be an effective means of communication. But you should pay attention to how well the animation is suited to the purpose you have in mind, and observe whether it is integrated with the rest of the page or whether it tears the whole thing apart.

First, you should examine the GIF. Important questions include: Does the sequence of the animation make sense? Is the timing between frames correct? How will it display when loading over a slower connection?

Answering these questions is not easy. The best method is to view the image over a modem connection to get a better feel for what the typical end user might see. One trick that may help improve display over slow connections is to begin your animation with a transparent frame with a delay of 3-10 seconds after it. This delay gives the browser time to preload subsequent frames so that they play back more smoothly when displayed.

Second, you should examine the relationship between your animated GIF and the rest of the page. Does the GIF distract your readers from the rest of the content? Does it loop unnecessarily?

Always bear in mind that although you want to draw attention to the content being presented in your animation, your users may be coming in search of other content. As much as you may be proud of your animation prowess, your readers may only find it annoying, like a little brother who keeps tapping on your shoulder.

Finally, you should think twice before using more than one animated GIF on a single page. Animated GIFs tend to say "Look at me!" in a loud voice. Unless they are carefully tuned to work together to achieve a common goal, using two or more animated GIFs on a single page is almost certain to create a shouting match that sends your users running with their ears covered.

Remember that in the end, enhancements should truly enhance your site and not exclude people from having the best possible visitor experience.

It is also important to have a thorough understanding of the technology before you dive in and try to implement it. Let's talk about the commonly interchanged Java and JavaScript. Although the names sound very similar, it's important to understand that there are fundamental differences between these two technologies.

Java is a full-featured programming language: it uses typed variables, has built-in methods of creating interface elements (such as windows), and is compiled into byte-code before execution. Java is attuned to building complex, independent, full-featured applications. To program in Java, you benefit greatly from prior experience programming in C or C++.

JavaScript, as its name implies, is a scripting language designed to work within an HTML document to manipulate elements of a page. JavaScript was originally introduced under the moniker LiveScript, but Netscape quickly realized it could capitalize on the popularity of Java by renaming its product. Although it borrows many of its conventions from Java and C++, JavaScript is dependent on the browser and lacks much of the power of those languages. JavaScript is entirely interpreted, rather than being compiled before execution. And although JavaScript can be quite complex, its scope of capabilities is far smaller and simpler than Java. One of the advantages of JavaScript is that users familiar with HTML can get started using it with no programming experience whatsoever, but it helps!

It is also important to understand that the Java and JavaScript are not inherently competing technologies. Although you may choose one or the other for a given project, the two can be used in conjunction. In particular, JavaScript provides ways to control browser behavior that may complement your Java applet. Also, JavaScript can be used to link Java applets to each other, serving as bridge to pass information between them. You can, for example, use JavaScript to trigger an action in one applet based on information from another applet.

PLUGGING IT IN

Although with some effort you can build dynamic, interactive sites using just HTML, there are some circumstances where you may want to look for more powerful ways of entertaining users. Since the development of plug-in-capable browsers, dynamic content delivery has taken on a myriad of new forms.

Arguably, one of the most popular plug-ins is Macromedia's Shockwave for Director. Director has long been the authoring tool of choice for multimedia artists and CD-ROM developers. Shockwave leveraged that popularity by enabling Director's users to rapidly port their dynamic content to the web using a highly compressed format geared to the lower data rates typical of the Internet.

Macromedia has continually improved on Shockwave since its inception. One of the more recent revisions added the ability to stream audio so that users could start hearing a sound file before it had finished downloading. Coupling this with Director's capability to create custom interfaces, Adjacency developed the Specialized Soundtrack—a Shockwave feature that enables the user to choose from a number of songs (see Figure 4.4). The Soundtrack console floats in a small window so that the user can "groove" while browsing the rest of the site.

Figure 4.4

The Macromedia's Shockwave plug-in has suc-ceeded for the best reasons—it's powerful, versa-tile, and useful. Adjacency's Specialized web site once featured a Shockwave-based site soundtrack.

The uses for Shockwave are innumerable. If you have extremely dynamic content that you want to build into your site, such as an interactive presentation or an online game, but have no idea how you would create it in HTML, consider creating it with Shockwave for Director instead. Although the learning curve is somewhat steep, Director has a rich development environment and mature scripting language to control all the elements of your project.

The major drawback of using plug-in-based solutions such as Shockwave is that because of their dependence on plug-ins, they tend to exclude users. Before investing your time in building a Shockwave feature, you must determine if your users will go to the trouble of downloading and installing the plug-ins required. Fortunately, since it was first introduced, the popularity of Shockwave has risen dramatically, so many of your users may already have the plug-in installed. This concern may also be minimized by the advent of "AutoInstall" technology, which promises to enable users to dynamically download, install, and load plug-ins with a minimum of fuss and without restarting the browser. Both Netscape and Microsoft claim to be building this capability into the next releases of their browsers. Put that on your technology-to-watch list.

If you can afford the time and effort, it's a good idea to provide gateways to an enhanced version as well as a "lite" version of the site. This way, your site can continue to grow and incorporate enhanced features without leaving some of your user base behind. Sometimes new technologies can achieve your objectives better than previous methods. Macromedia Flash, for instance, enables you to create complex streaming, interactive animations that have amazingly small file sizes. When Akimbo Design developed a Flash movie for their home page, it turned out to be only 12K compared with the animated GIF version that amounted to 33K. Imagine slashing the file sizes of your animations in half! Your animations can include buttons with customized rollovers and sound effects as well as multiple scenes. Because Flash uses vector-based technology, you can use your favorite fonts for your text without worrying about a user's system fonts. To top it off, Flash movies scale within changing browser window sizes! Keep in mind that users need to download the Macromedia Shockwave plug-in to view Flash movies. So, until most users have browsers that can automatically download special plug-ins, it's best to provide an "unplugged" version of your site along with the enhanced version. We don't want to discourage you from using cool technologies; we simply want to help you make sure that you use the right one for your message and your needs. Then, when you decide what to use, we hope you remember to accommodate your users who were a little late for the technology train.

GETTING FLASHY

One of the cooler new developments in web technology is Macromedia's Flash. The latest addition to the Shockwave series of browser enhancements, Flash brings much-needed innovation to the plug-in arena. Flash is a means of delivering animation and user interactivity similar in many ways to Shockwave for Director.

Where most of the elements in Shockwave for Director are pixel-based, with a fixed size and resolution, Flash stores all of its elements as vector data, similar to drawing programs such as Illustrator or FreeHand. This enables elements to be scaled to any size without appearing jaggy. This also reduces the file size overhead for many animations, as the same vector information can be used to render an element in different locations and at different sizes over time. This innovation alone makes Flash a compelling piece of technology.

Originally developed by FutureWave software under the name FutureSplash, the tool received the name Flash when Macromedia acquired FutureWave. Now entering the beta testing phase for version 2 at the time of this writing, Flash has seen many improvements under Macromedia's ownership. The development environment has been revised to follow the user interface guidelines used by other Macromedia apps such as Director and SoundEdit Pro (see Figure 4.5). Macromedia also added sound support, giving developers the ability to import sound into their animations and trigger it based on user interaction. Expect to see Flash-enabled sites popping up all over the web in the months to come. Perhaps one of them will be yours.

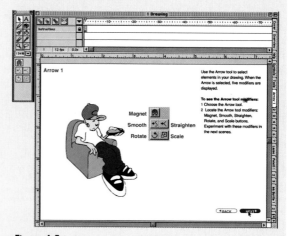

Figure 4.5

The Flash Editor is immediately familiar to users of Macromedia's other development tools.

For more examples of Flash at work, visit Macromedia's Shockzone at http://www.macro-media.com/shockzone/.

CREATING TANGIBLE RESULTS THROUGH INTERACTIVITY

We have mentioned before that you always need a reason—in fact, a good reason—for whatever you do on your site. Thus, the reasons for including certain interactive features should stem from your original site objectives and strategies. Site enhancements usually involve more than being cool or hip (unless of course this is your only objective). These interactive features, whether they are movies, submission forms, or searchable databases, should fulfill your objectives and reinforce your strategies. All parts of the site relate to each other. Your goals and your plans to fulfill these goals unify your message within the web interface.

Of course, the first step is routed in Chapter 2. If you haven't set clear objectives and strategies, go back and read that chapter! This particular chapter lays out the steps in turning your ideas into tangible interactive features for your web site that fulfill your overall site goals.

- ◆ Learn your client's business.
- ◆ Find out what user-derived information your client could use.
- ◆ Translate or enhance existing information, services, or programs.
- ◆ Entice users to compromise their anonymity.
- ◆ Spur users to action.
- ◆ Use visitor interaction to generate free, diverse site content.
- ◆ Enhance your navigational system.

LEARN YOUR CLIENT'S BUSINESS

Learn what advertising, sales, distribution, marketing, and communications models are. You need to understand the client from the consumer, from client factions, and from the media's point of view before, during, and after creating the web site. Ask questions. Research your client's business using such tools as the Wall Street Journal Interactive Edition and Lexus Nexus. You must keep track of their products—what's new, what sells the best. Inform your client that you need to be in the loop for any new developments within the company. Ask your client for any reports or internal documents that help you see the grand scheme of their goals and strategies. Make sure you participate in meetings that involve planning or brainstorming for new items to go up on the web site.

You need to expose yourself to all facets of the client's company to be involved in the development process. Give the corporate marketing and communications people the lead in terms of what you are working on, but find out what other departments' challenges are. Dig up the scoop on customer relations, customer service, and media relations. Figure out how you can solve some of those issues through the Internet. Work through the company's committees through your client contact. Create surveys that they can circulate internally. Offer case studies with problems you have encountered with other clients. These examples often light light bulbs and inspire them to re-evaluate their needs and concerns. The case study "Working with Your Client Beyond the Launch," in Chapter 6, deals with our relationship with Land Rover and how we communicate with each other in order to stay attuned to the company's evolving needs.

Understanding the bigger picture behind your client's company helps you make decisions about what interactive features to include on the site. You need to inform your client that the Internet often offers solutions to their problems. Too many people view the Internet as just another communications medium or at the other extreme, a panacea. The web is neither. Rather, it falls somewhere right in the middle.

FIND OUT WHAT USER-DERIVED INFORMATION YOUR CLIENT COULD USE

You need to talk with your client's marketing people to find out what consumer research they do, what they're interested in. If they could find out anything about their customers, what would it be? If you design a survey with a properly designed incentive structure, you may be able to convince your site visitors to volunteer that information, especially if you can convince them that volunteering the information is to their benefit. Offering individualized attention means improved service in general.

Most companies have a way for customers to communicate with them. You can use the web to facilitate this relationship so that customers can give feedback on previous purchases or order products, for example. Once the company commits to responding to emails, you must determine whether it can respond within two days. It's better not to do it than to do it poorly. Rollerblade's ability to respond within 24 or 48 hours to the previous 10,000 email inquiries—for anything ranging from sales to minor repairs—keeps existing customers happy. This response time and dedication also enables them to gain new customers and further their reputation for being a high customer relations company. The worst possible thing is for people to send an email and not get an email back.

In the competitor appraisal process, we often try other people's feedback forms. We have learned that most companies respond in over a week. A company should at all costs try to avoid anything like that from happening on its web site. In the Rollerblade project, we tried to make the email as direct as possible. With a pull-down menu to specify a particular subject, the feedback form sends a user's request directly to the person responsible for

the topic (see Figure 4.6). Refer to this section's sidebar, "Designing Forms," as well as our companion web site, `http://www.adj.com/ killer/`, for details and examples on how to implement effective forms.

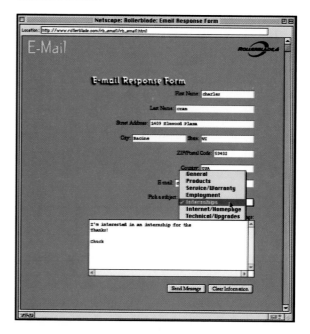

Figure 4.6

Rollerblade.com's email response form helps the user route their mail to the correct party by using a pull-down subject menu, provides the user with a confirmation that their mail was sent, and manages their expectations concerning response time.

DESIGNING FORMS

Asking users to fill out a form is not something that should be taken lightly. If you take as much of the work off their shoulders as possible, they are that more likely to fill out the form completely and accurately. To this end, you should design your forms in the same manner that you design any other part of the site—with an eye toward clear and logical presentation of information so that users know exactly what is expected of them.

The best tool on hand for making your forms clear and easily understandable is the <TABLE> tag. With the proper use of tables, you can ensure that your form elements line up as they might if they were printed on paper. In this way, the strong horizontals and verticals can be used to guide your users through the form so that they know exactly what to fill out next.

In addition to organizing the individual elements, you might consider breaking out a longer form over multiple pages so that your users can fill it out in smaller, more easily consumable chunks. This involves passing variables along to the new form, a technique that is outside the scope of this book. If this is not an option for you, consider dividing your form into sections using horizontal rules.

You might also consider complementing your form with graphic elements that aid the user in understanding what the form is asking for. These can range in complexity from a simple header GIF to miniature icons or graphics illustrating particular parts of the form. The key here is to use only what is absolutely necessary; too much may only serve to confuse your design and frustrate the user.

Finally, another nice touch you can add to your form is a simple, subtle background color. This makes your form elements stand out a little better, further aiding readability and accenting your organization.

Figures 4.7 and 4.8 show a form before and after these principles have been applied.

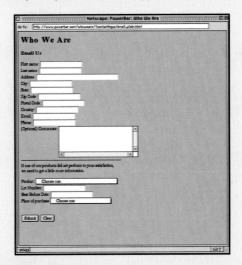

Figure 4.7

Though functional, a web form in its unformatted, undesigned, hypertext-only state is not very approachable.

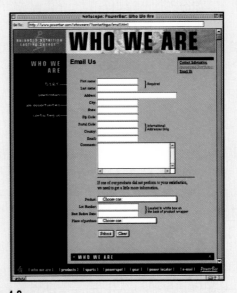

Figure 4.8

Presentation is everything. Orderly layout and attention to detail make a form user-friendly.

TRANSLATE OR ENHANCE EXISTING INFORMATION, SERVICES, OR PROGRAMS

Challenge yourself to determine the best way to display information intuitively and quickly. You cannot simply repurpose print, broadcasting, and other kinds of existing materials, tempting and obvious as it may seem. At the same, time you should not be seduced by the rapidly changing web technology. Tips and tricks only help you when they enable your web site's clearly defined goals to be met. You need to understand the web medium—what works and what doesn't.

Here is an overview of what a company can apply to its web site and incorporate as interactive features:

- **Anything database-driven.** Web-deployed databases with well-designed user interfaces enable users to search large amounts of information quickly and consistently. The classic example of this is the online dealer locator.
- **Anything tied into the company's back-end computer system.** Powerful legacy integration packages such as Apple Computer's WebObjects enable companies to quickly and rather inexpensively tie such processes as online ordering and fulfillment to a web interface. Many companies with traditional mail order programs are finding that their web facilitated sales are much more efficient and, hence, higher margin than toll free telephone or postal mail ordering.
- **Digital files.** The moment you have video, photographic, animated, or audio content converted into ones and zeros, you are presented with the opportunity to change the way people interact with it. You can deploy those files in a way that enables users to control how they consume that information. Instead of simply playing or displaying those files, you can allow users the chance to control their exposure to it. Allowing users to start, stop, and skip forward and back seems simple enough, but many visitors appreciate that added power. At its simplest level, it's like the difference between watching a movie broadcast on television and watching that broadcast after its recorded onto a videocassette. Watching the latter, you're able to scan through the "document" in search of the experience or information you're after.
- **Anything reduced to an electronic or digital transaction.** Information gathering and digital automation are the time and cost-saving patron saints of the web. Take an email form for example. A well-designed email form enables you to consistently ask individuals for information in exactly the same words, in exactly the same order every time. You're not paying a person to sit at a telephone and transpose the information. What's more, the email form is open for business all day, every day.
- **Anything transmitted over phone lines.** In short, you can use a web site to disseminate and collect any type of information or content that can be reduced to or converted into digital information. The only limitation is the bandwidth of the network or connection between the people or organizations on either end.

As you can see, the options span a wide gamut of examples. To be of any use, they must be organized and packaged in such a way that people can access them easily and conveniently through the web interface that you design. Again, we recommend that you take an interdisciplinary approach to design where you think in terms of a designer, a programmer, a marketer, a sales person, and, most importantly, a consumer. The following is a list of the general services or programs that work well in the web medium:

◆ Product ordering
◆ Customer support
◆ Customer feedback
◆ Contests or promotions
◆ Product selection or recommendation features
◆ Retailer referrals
◆ Product demos

After you determine the information, services, or programs that you want to include on your site, you need to know the different options and avenues to follow. Here are some general examples of web interactive features.

◆ **Submission forms** include email contact forms, feedback forms, and forms that enable users to submit text and graphics. Basic forms provide simple communication between the user and the company, whereby the user makes his or her submission and expects a response within a reasonable amount of time. These types of forms work best when you build in an automatic response page that comes up immediately after a submission to reassure the user that his or her input has successfully gone through the wires. The next level of forms generate results dynamically. Right away, the user can see how they have added or

manipulated content on your web site. The World Ride Web directory on the Specialized site enables users to add their submissions instantly to a growing list of bike trails from all over the world.

◆ **Searchable databases** include site search engines, retailer locators, and special directories such as the World Ride Web area. These databases add convenience to the user experience as well as to your maintenance procedures. You enable users to find exactly what they are looking for with intelligent and comprehensive search features, while automating the site updates for yourself. Further into this chapter you discover that you can, in fact, spur users to action by providing such things as a dealer locator. You provide next steps for your users and eliminate the need for them to ask, "Now what?" because you have already laid out the path for them to walk out the door to the nearest retailer. Refer to the "Spur to Action" section for more information on developing a dealer locator.

◆ **Graphical interactive features** include Java, JavaScript rollovers, and Shockwave games. These features enable users to manipulate and actively change some part of the interface. Through Java applets and JavaScript rollovers, you can create effective graphical navigational elements that respond to a user's wandering mouse path. When a user scans over a web page, the mouse usually follows this person's eyes. If a button changes color or if explanation text pops up as the mouse passes over a clickable item, you provide more hints as to where the user can go from there. Another effective use of

Java applets is for an interface whose individual parts change according to a user's selections. In one of this chapter's case studies, "Outfit Your Land Rover," you see how we used such an applet on the Land Rover site to enable users to see what different vehicle models looked like with certain colors and accessories. Finally, Shockwave provides a means to combine complex and clever graphics, sounds, and game-like interactivity into one animated movie. Now that you can stream large Shockwave movies, you can bring more of a sensational look and entertaining feel to your web sites. Refer to this chapter's sidebars, "Implementing Image Link Rollovers," and "Plugging It In," for more information on graphical interactive features.

◆ **Individualized site presentation** involves the site recognizing a user and responding to him or her specifically. Personalization can be as basic as recognizing a user's platform and browser in order to display the appropriate version of your site or as complex as greeting users by name each time he or she visits your site. Either way, we should all strive to achieve some degree of site personalization in order to create better interactive web sites. Our case study on personalizing PowerBar's site and our sidebar on cookies give you a better idea of what it takes to create an individualized site presentation.

◆ **Movies and soundtracks** enable users to stop, start, and play sounds and animations. These features are more passive forms of interactivity but are still interactive to the point that you must consciously activate certain actions. Again, we encourage you to check out the sidebar "Plugging It In" to get a better handle for implementing special technologies that enable you to play movies and soundtracks on your web site.

In any given implementation of an interactive feature to your web site, you should be prepared to invest in some sort of automation system. Receiving tons of information, requests, and feedback from your users is great for your ego that's always worried about site traffic, but if you or your client don't have the power to respond to your audience in a timely manner, then you defeat the purpose of having an interactive web site. Remember that interactivity is a two-way street. Automation through databases, cookies, and scripts generates dynamic web site content in an efficient and manageable manner. Unless you use some form of automation, you are faced with the burden of creating your site entirely by hand. Your life will become miserable and your audience will feel neglected. Your technical team should be able to handle the cookies and special scripts to generate dynamic pages and route specific email requests. Special software systems are also available that enable you to create templates and plug-in content without having to worry about formatting or uploading. Chapter 6 provides more helpful hints on how to maintain your site through automation.

ENTICE USERS TO COMPROMISE THEIR ANONYMITY

Your ultimate goal is to keep your users as customers and give them better service. In order to achieve and maintain this relationship, you need to convince them that you are a trustworthy company and would never share the personal information they have volunteered. Be forthright about why you are interested in their ideas and their answers to your questions. If you value your customers, you need to demonstrate that this information will enable you to serve them better.

The ultimate goal of all marketers on the web is to know how many people are hitting the site and who they are. Site personalization features enable you to collect demographic and psychographic profiles. Users appreciate site personalization because it saves time by showing them only the information relevant to their needs and interests.

They are treated as an individual, not as an anonymous user.

Such assurances regarding improved services are not always enough, however. Some people want a more tangible exchange. People are willing to provide basic information about themselves, their purchasing habits, and their attitudes about your company and the industry in general, in exchange for even the possibility of winning a sweepstakes, saving money on their next purchase, getting extra support, getting individualized customer service or product support, and of course, getting free stuff.

POWERBAR: PERSONALIZING YOUR SITE FOR DIFFERENT USERS

The future of web sites and online information delivery and interaction in general lies in further customizing presentation to individual's personal interests and needs. PowerBar's PowerUser feature is a system that selectively presents site information to consumers based on individualized user profiles. In essence, users are presented with their own private PowerBar.com.

To register to become a PowerUser, a site visitor fills out an online questionnaire that enables them to indicate the sports they are interested in, their gender, where they live, and other details that describe them and their interests. Using this information, a customized site menu is generated that welcomes them back each time they visit the site. PowerUsers can personalize this menu, adding links to their favorite sports sections within the site. Their site menu also informs them if any content has been added to their favorite sports sections since their last visit (see Figures 4.9 and 4.10).

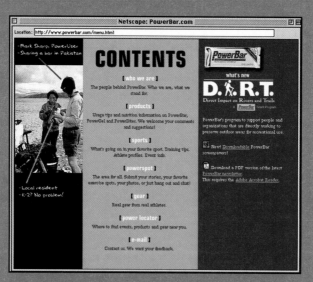

Figure 4.9

The standard PowerBar.com site menu organizes all of the site's content into a manageable list of options people can use to locate what they're after.

Figure 4.10

PowerBar.com's PowerUser feature uses user survey responses to create a site menu customized to that individual's personal profile that includes their interests and location. In essence, a lot of the information they're after steps forward to greet them.

The PowerUser also has the ability to give input on the development of the site through an online suggestion box, accessible from their personal site menu. We found PowerUser input to be invaluable in approaching the first major redesign of the site, so we decided to get input from them on a more regular basis.

In addition to these features, PowerUsers are also eligible for monthly PowerBar product and gear giveaways. They can create private chat rooms and post messages to a PowerUser-only bulletin board. PowerUsers also have the opportunity to be profiled on the site, with their photo showing on the site menu for all site visitors to see.

Through site personalization, we create an infinite number of sites from one site. Users are addressed as individuals and not as a massive, nameless, faceless audience. Targeted messages can be created for our users because we know who they are and what they need. We try to obtain as much demographic information as possible in order to create a direct dialog with consumers. Through this dialog, we can mature and develop the site according to their needs. We learn more about them as they learn more about the brand. The site visitors become loyal users who recommend the site—and the product—to others.

SPUR USERS TO ACTION

The more you minimize and eliminate uncertainty in your message, the more you can lead a consumer to a certain action, especially if it is to make a purchase decision. Guided audio tour descriptions of products and services as well as QuickTime VR movies are great ways for the user to get as close to the showroom experience as possible (see Figure 4.11).

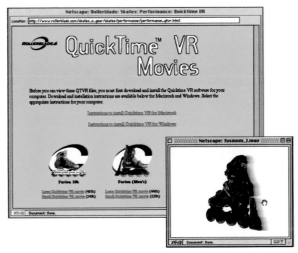

Figure 4.11

Why limit your presentation of products in a dynamic medium such as the web to static images? Rollerblade.com uses QuickTime VR technology to give consumers 360-degree views of the skates.

At some point, users will want to go beyond the information in a brochure. They will want to go to the dealer or to the store to see, touch, smell, and at times, taste the product. Your responsibility in creating the web site is to help them make as many decisions as possible before seeing the actual car, tasting the nutritional bar, or putting on the inline skates. You need to create the illusion that they can totally visualize, manipulate, and handle the product. Therefore, choosing interactive features that enable users to imagine themselves using the products helps convince them that this product is right for them and motivate them to go out and use or buy the product or service.

LAND ROVER: OUTFIT YOUR LAND ROVER

When we created the Land Rover site, we did not have the resources the first time around to create an interactive car customization or selection feature. When we finally did create it during the next phase of the site design (`http://www.landrover.com/features/outfit/`), we blew the competition away (see Figure 4.12)!

Figure 4.12

The Outfit Your Land Rover feature offers users a fast, graphical way to experiment with different vehicle models, colors and vehicle kit items. What's more, it provides Land Rover with valuable market research.

We had a photographer take shots of different Land Rover vehicles with different combinations of accessories. We then used Photoshop to re-create the vehicles in all of the available colors and created transparent GIFs of each of the accessories. Using Java, we set up an interface to "Outfit Your Land Rover" that enabled users, in an instant, to view different models with different extras added on. Users can now get to the site and see their preferred vehicle in the available exterior and interior colors. Depending on the model, racks, a running board, chrome plating, headlight protectors, and any combination of these options could be added.

Outfit Your Land Rover stands to be an interactive application or feature that people can always use. It brings the showroom experience closer to the prospective buyer or customer and leaves very little to the imagination of users. They can see exactly what their options are.

In addition, we allow users to print out the final options they selected so that they can take this specific information to the dealer (see Figure 4.13). Approximately 250 people go so far as to print their options every day.

Figure 4.13

After customizing their favorite Land Rover vehicle, the user can view and print a summary of what they've selected.

In creating a web site, we strive to keep ahead of the technology and don't let it seduce us into using random bells and whistles on a site for technology's sake. We address a need and determine the best possible means for executing the idea. In Outfit Your Land Rover, Java was determined to be the best tool for swapping images in a custom selection interface. We didn't sit down and try to figure out what would be the best way to use Java on the Land Rover site. The ideas and useful applications drove the design and development of a site, not technological techniques and tricks.

Although you may design the best and the coolest product simulation on the web, you still need to plan for user questions. Make sure that a contact form link is highly visible and accessible so that people can request any additional information. Provide an area for frequently asked questions (FAQs) so that people can understand and relate to the product through common concerns shared by other people (see Figure 4.14).

 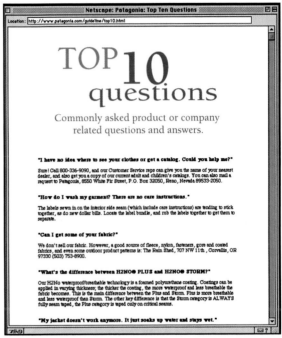

Figure 4.14

Patagonia knows menus of frequently asked questions are helpful for the site visitor who doesn't have time to scour the site or send an email inquiry and sit tight. This is equally helpful for the site manager who would otherwise have to respond to the visitor's email inquiry.

Now that you have provided product information, you must make it convenient and easy for people to find, locate, and purchase the product. A dealer locator does that if it is well designed. If you are building a site for a national brand name, your client most likely wants to provide users with a means to find the location nearest them that stocks its brand. This sort of interactive feature is typically known as a dealer locator.

The simplest form of dealer locator would be a list of dealer names with their locations and phone numbers. But to the designer who strives to bring interactivity to the fore, this solution is clearly weak and unprofessional.

A better solution is to provide users with an interactive means of telling you where they live and using that information to provide them with the location of the dealer nearest them. This can be done visually using a clickable map of the country or region that encompasses all of the brand's dealers (see Figure 4.15). When the user clicks her region, the server compiles a list of locations from a database and serves them a custom-built page containing that information.

Figure 4.15

Patagonia's web site uses a map-based dealer locator. It's an involved but handsome visual solution that enables users to find retailers by city. This is helpful when there are many dealers in your immediate ZIP code or when a dealer in an adjacent ZIP code is closer than those in your own.

Another way of achieving the same thing would be to have the user enter his or her ZIP code (see Figure 4.16). This is less visual, but at the same time, it returns more specific information, which may be more useful to the user. One drawback to this method is that it requires that all the dealers be in the same country and that the user also live in that country.

In addition to interactive features that make the user experience more informative and convenient, site individualization is another way to convince users that your product is exactly what they need. Making the user experience fast and exciting is one thing. Welcoming users by name even after they haven't visited the site in a while and introducing a new product or event they might be interested in are other things that take the site to the next level. By making the site less anonymous, you demonstrate to users that you are dedicated to making them happy. You are dedicated to customer service and support and care about who your users are and what they want. Add-ons can be recommended based on what you know they want, thus minimizing the purchase consideration time.

Figure 4.16

Land Rover's online dealer locator uses a combination of postal codes and geographical regions in its dealer locator. The dealer locator tends to be a faster search method, but it is best used when dealer locations are geographically spread-out.

137

USING COOKIES TO PERSONALIZE YOUR SITE

Cookies serve as a mechanism by which server-side connections, such as CGI scripts, store and retrieve information on the client side of the connection. (The word "cookie" does not serve as a fancy acronym for this tool. It's just a name.) By using cookies, web sites can re-use registration information and free users from re-identifying themselves or restating preferences. The most common cookie application stores the username and password necessary to access a password-protected site. In Internet commerce, shopping applications can now store customer selections in a "shopping basket" no matter where he or she navigates within the site, keeping track of selections and rejections. Major "cookie-capable" browsers include Netscape Navigator, Microsoft Internet Explorer, Emissary/Wollongong, and Oracle PowerBrowser.

You can use cookies to:

◆ **Store information about a user.** With cookies, you can ask for user input and store this information: name, email address, and so on.

◆ **Recall information about a user.** Tapping into this stored information, you can personalize your site for your user.

◆ **Personalize your web site without using CGI scripts.** You can create cookies with JavaScript without the hassle of extra server connections.

Many people have huge misconceptions about cookies and may feel threatened by them. They feel that cookies invade their privacy by creating a preferences file on their computers. The fact is, cookies are specific to the web pages or web sites that use them. No one else can access these files. No one can take information from cookies that they did not already put there. Cookies have no actual power. They are files that a server or browser can work with and store information for use at a later date. In fact, cookies can store only a limited amount of information—approximately 20K. Cookies do not damage other files on your hard drive nor do they extract information from your computer that you would not be willing to volunteer. Servers and browsers can already do that without the help of cookies. Cookies simply store information.

Unfortunately, there is no way to effectively dispel myths about cookies other than general web education and awareness. Web surfers need to understand and appreciate that cookies can store your preferences pertaining to a particular site. Each time you visit a site with cookies, you get the personalized attention and information that simplifies your web experience.

Think of each web page as a doorway or window into your world. By using cookies that recognize your specific users, you can welcome your audience with your own flair and style within a personalized interface.

The ultimate next step in a corporate web site is online commerce. If someone sees a product, has read the FAQ, and decides right then that he wants to buy, he should be able to click a button to order. It should be a simple step to complete a form and get the product within a couple of days or at most a week. Most corporate web sites endeavor to inform consumers about their products to inspire future purchases. If you can take this soft sell approach a step further and actually enable users to purchase directly, then you have completed the loop. As with any other feature included on your site, only implement it if you can truly follow through and execute. To make online commerce a success much like a regular retail operation, you need to be able to offer secure transactions, ensure reliable fulfillment of the orders, manage your inventory, and create promotional sales. Clearly, the issues go beyond the scope of this book. Just know that online commerce is another option that might take care site to the next level, but it is definitely not mandatory in creating a killer interactive web site.

USE VISITOR INTERACTION TO GENERATE FREE, DIVERSE SITE CONTENT

The coolest and best interactive features are the ones that perpetuate themselves. When we started the World Ride Web trail directory for Specialized, we seeded it with 100 trails and then encouraged cycling web surfers to add their own. We asked them, "What's your favorite?" In a few months, we had over 600 trails on the list, and it continues to grow today. Such an interactive feature shows that you know about the site's subject matter—in this case, the sport of biking—and demonstrates that you are an expert. You're real. You're hard-core. You're creating and fostering a community, showing the audience that you are a consumer just like them. These kinds of features show that you want to learn about the audience and truly desire two-way communication.

POWERSPOT: CREATING AND FOSTERING AN ONLINE COMMUNITY

In addition to providing personalized attention through site customization, the PowerBar site sought to create and foster an online community among its users. Building a sense of community in a web site adds value to the web experience. Users feel connected to other people by engaging in an active exchange of ideas and information.

We decided to develop the "PowerSpot" (`http://www.powerbar.com/powerspot/`) submission area to develop this sense of community on the site (see Figure 4.17). Visitors have the opportunity to submit stories or "Tales of Optimum Performance" about their personal exercising experiences. People are encouraged to submit anything from prose to poetry to describe their experiences that are not necessarily related to the PowerBar product. Visitors can also submit photographs to the photo gallery. You can share a picture of yourself climbing a mountain, swimming across the English Channel, shooting some hoops at your neighborhood playground, sailing on the San Francisco Bay, weightlifting in Venice Beach, or playing Laser Tag in the comfort of your own home (see Figure 4.18).

Figure 4.17

PowerBar.com's PowerSpot is the hub of the online community that has developed there.

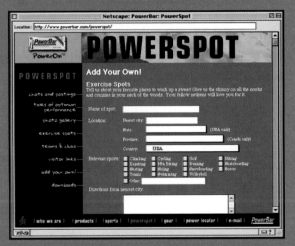

Figure 4.18

Visitors to PowerBar.com share information in the form of stories, photos, and a directory of favorite exercise spots through use of an online submission form.

We invite people to submit their favorite places to exercise all around the world. This list includes different sports in different places. The list provides quick descriptions of the sport and place as well as directions on how to get there. This database-driven feature enables visitors to search by country, state or province, and type of exercise to get comprehensive lists of people's submissions. The PowerSpot area also provides localized content where visitors can submit local club listings. If there is a group that gets together every Friday night for Frisbee golf in Seattle, for example, or another group that skates through the streets of San Francisco, their listings show up in this area of the site.

On a larger scale, PowerBar sponsors 50 to 100 athletes and over 4,000 sporting events per year. Each country hosts approximately five or six events each day. PowerBar tracks the athletes' performance and results from these major events. As part of their contracts, these sponsored athletes are responsible for a certain amount of content generation for the web site. Each athlete has his or her own section where the athlete contributes columns and pictures for their individual sports. In addition, the web site provides athlete profiles, tips from the pros, and regularly updated stories that enable amateur enthusiasts to benefit from different perspectives.

Triathlete Cameron Widoff has a "Cam's Eye View" section where he provides a feature story on a regular basis. He has an email address available to PowerSpot users so that they can communicate directly with him. A threaded discussion connected to "Cam's Eye View" enables users to interact with each other. Chat rooms, a posting board, and threaded discussions enable visitors to respond to one of the existing topics or add your own topic and start a discussion.

In effect, the PowerSpot fosters a community among PowerBar users, from complete recreational users to professional, sponsored athletes.

Using content generated by site visitors and users gives them a sense of ownership. Adjacency credits users in their submissions. When we let them leave their mark, they feel like a valued part of the site because of their contributions. Whether creating a forum for discussion in chat rooms or setting up a directory of a user's favorite whatevers, you are creating something that dynamically updates itself. When people see that their ideas are valued, appreciated, and honored, they continue to use the site because of this sense of ownership. They are also interested to see other people's comments and submissions and regard the site as a place for people with names, faces, and personalities. Remember that designing and developing a web site means creating a web application that provides useful and interesting information that customers can use to enrich their lives.

ENHANCE YOUR NAVIGATIONAL SYSTEM

One of the simplest, most basic places you can integrate interactive features on your site is within your navigational system. Users necessarily interact with your navigation to get the information they want. The more intuitive and useful it is, the happier and more rewarded the user is.

Rollovers are the most popular way to enhance navigation. You can achieve a rollover effect with static images using JavaScript or Java, whereas technologies such as Shockwave create the effect in multimedia movies or animations. A rollover can be as simple as showing a personalized message in the status bar of the browser or as sophisticated as having a highlight or drop shadow show up when the cursor passes over the image. Rollovers make the navigation look like navigation. They make your navigational elements look clickable and functional. Rollovers also provide instant feedback to a user's actions. In a sense, a rollover recognizes that the user has selected or is about to select a certain area.

Rollovers also help users focus on each navigational element individually. The rollover effect compartmentalizes each area of the navigation and draws the user's attention to individual elements one at a time. Therefore, the rollover effect enhances the usefulness of the navigation without detracting from the overall layout and design of the page. People only see this special effect when they need to use the navigation.

This brings up a crucial point. You cannot rely on a rollover effect to make your navigation useful. The design of the navigation has to be strong enough on its own to be effective. Rollovers are design enhancements, not solutions. People have to find and use the navigation for the first time before they know there is a rollover effect. Be sure to check out our detailed sidebar on image link rollovers in this section for specific examples.

IMPLEMENTING IMAGE LINK ROLLOVERS

One of the easiest ways to give users interactive feedback is to have links respond in some way to their actions. Not so long ago, the only way this was possible was to specify a VLINK color for followed links so that links the users had already visited would differentiate themselves from unfollowed links. With the advent of JavaScript 1.1, this interaction becomes more dynamic—and immediate—through the use of image link rollovers.

THE IMAGES ARRAY

In a JavaScript 1.1-compliant browser, information about the images in the current document is stored in an array called *document.images*. This is a list of the images in the order they appear in the HTML source with some descriptive information attached to each image:

The Images Array

Name	Number	SRC
news_button	0	images/news button.gif
clients_button	1	images/clients button.gif
jobs_button	2	images/jobs button.gif
links_button	3	images/links button.gif
tools_button	4	images/tools button.gif

The actual array contains much more information than shown in this table, but this illustrates the basic idea. By using information in this array, we can manipulate the images in the current document in many ways. For our purposes, the most important piece of information about each image is its SRC, which is short for source. By changing the source for a given image, we can swap a new image in its place. This is the basis for implementing image link rollovers.

To change an image's source, we need to specify which image we want to manipulate. The simplest way to refer to an image in the array is by number. `document.images[0]`, for example, refers to the first image in the document, as JavaScript counts from zero. Thus, `document.images[1]` refers to the second image, and so on. Given this, we can change an image's source by giving the command

```
document.images[0].src = 'new_image.gif';
```

inserting the path to your new image on the right side of the equation.

Unfortunately, if you are building a page that uses multiple rollovers within a complicated layout, referring to images by number can become tedious and may lead to errors. To alleviate this problem, JavaScript enables us to give images a NAME attribute so we can refer to them using this name and bypass the numbering business altogether. If, for example, we insert an image using

```
<IMG       SRC="images/news_button.gif"
BORDER=0 NAME="news_button">
```

we can then refer to the image as `document.images['news_button']`. Thus, to change its source, we can simply enter

```
document.images['news_button'].src    =
'news_button_active.gif';
```

and avoid the confusion of referring to images by number.

BUILDING A FUNCTION

To execute these commands, it is best to place them within a function at the beginning of the document so that they can be called from anywhere else in the document. A function is basically a list of actions grouped together and given a name so they can be executed as a whole. A function has a certain structure that may at first appear confusing, but on closer examination, has some interesting logic to it:

```
function news_button_swap() {
      document.images['news_button'].src =
'images/news_button_active.gif';
}
```

This is simply the command we described earlier, enclosed in some curly brackets, preceded by the word `function` and the name of the function. This basically says, "If the function `news_button_swap` is called, then change the source of `news_button` to `news_button_active.gif`."

This function, however, only enables us to change the source of a particular image, `news_button`. This function can be made more modular by telling it which image we want to swap when the function is called:

```
function image_swap(image_name) {
      document.images[image_name].src  =
'images/' + image_name + '_active.gif';
}
```

Here we are passing a value to the function, using the variable `image_name`, so that the function can refer to the value as it executes the commands. If we trigger the function by saying

```
image_swap('news_button')
```

the browser executes the command

```
document.images['news_button'].src     =
'images/' + 'news_button' + '_active.gif';
```

which is another way of saying

```
document.images['news_button'].src     =
'images/news_button_active.gif';
```

which is what we started with. But if we pass it the value `clients_button`, the function swaps a different image entirely.

To restore an image, we use a very similar function:

```
function image_restore(image_name) {
      document.images[image_name].src   =
'images/' + image_name + '.gif';
}
```

Note that we are not adding `_active` to the filename in this case.

These functions require some uniformity in the way we name our images. For each image, we have a regular version and an active version. The regular news button, `news_button.gif`, for example, is accompanied by an active version that we name `news_button_active.gif`. Thus, to swap in an active version of any given image, we simply add `_active` to the filename or omit it to restore the original.

These functions are custom-defined, so you can name them whatever you want. They should be placed at the beginning of your document, within a special <SCRIPT> container between the <HEAD> tags:

```
<HTML>
<HEAD>
<TITLE>Site Menu</TITLE>
<SCRIPT LANGUAGE="JavaScript">

function image_swap(image_name) {
      document.images[image_name].src  =
'images/' + image_name + '_active.gif';
}

function image_restore(image_name) {
      document.images[image_name].src  =
'images/' + image_name + '.gif';
}
</SCRIPT>
</HEAD>
```

BRING IN THE USER

Now that we know how to swap an image's source, we need to explore how to activate the swap based on user interaction.

JavaScript enables us to monitor certain user actions through the use of event handlers. Event handlers are basically triggers that we can set to initiate an event based on the user's behavior.

To create an image rollover we make use of two JavaScript event handlers, `onMouseover` and `onMouseout`. These handlers enable us to trigger an action when the user points at an image (`onMouseover`) and when the user moves the cursor away from an image (`onMouseout`).

```
<A HREF="news.html"
    onMouseover="image_swap('news_button')"
        onMouseout="image_restore('news_
button')">
<IMG    SRC="news_button.gif"    BORDER=0
NAME="news_button"></A>
```

Here we have an image, `news_button.gif`, that is being defined as a link to news.html. (Note that the event handlers are added to the `<A HREF>` tag, and not the `<IMG>` tag. This is because event handlers can be triggered only by links, not just any page element. Although this has its disadvantages, it does enable us to trigger events when the user points at text links as well as image links.) When the user points at `news_button.gif`, the browser executes the JavaScript function `image_swap`, highlighting the image, and when the mouse is moved elsewhere, it executes `image_restore`, causing the image to return to normal (see Figures 4.19 and 4.20).

Figure 4.19

Specialized's World Ride Web v.4.0 Platinum was one of Adjacency's first sites to use JavaScript rollovers extensively. In this screen shot, everything on the page is calm...

Figure 4.20

...until the cursor passes over a link, at which point all hell breaks lose.

YOU BREAK IT, YOU BOUGHT IT

Unfortunately, this cool new feature of JavaScript does not work with every browser. In fact, as of this writing Netscape Navigator 3 and 4 and Internet Explorer 4 are the only browsers that support it. If anyone tries to view this page with other browsers, they may encounter an error (see Figure 4.21).

Figure 4.21

Some older browsers don't know what the docu-ment.images array is, causing an error.

Fortunately, there is a way to foolproof these func-tions so that other browsers can view the same page without complications.

Many site designers make use of a JavaScript object called `navigator`, which has a property called `appVersion`. By checking the value of `nav-igator.appVersion`, we can tell which browser the user is running and what version. This is com-plicated and actually quite unnecessary for our purposes. As you can see from the previous screen shot, the problem is simply that this browser does not have an array called `docu-ment.images`. Knowing this, all we need to do is check for the existence of the `document.images` array before trying to use it. Thus, our functions need to be only slightly modified:

```
function image_swap(image_name) {
    if (document.images){
        document.images[image_name].src =
'images/' + image_name + '_active.gif';
```

```
    }
}

function image_restore(image_name) {
    if (document.images){
        document.images[image_name].src =
'images/' + image_name + '.gif';
    }
}
```

If these functions are called while running an older browser, they check to see if `document.images` exists, and failing that, ignore the rest of the func-tion. The beauty of this solution is that as other browsers come into compliance with JavaScript 1.1, this code does not have to be modified at all.

Try using the previously defined functions in a document of your own. Experiment with different ways of highlighting the link images using Photoshop or your favorite image editor. Try to imagine other uses of image swapping, such as swapping in text GIFs to give the illusion of con-text-sensitive help. There is a lot that can be done with this simple tool.

For more information on JavaScript rollovers and related issues, such as preloading images, please visit the companion book site at http://www.adj.com/killer/.

You might also want to address the segment of your audience who feels compelled to circumvent your well-designed navigation on your well-designed site. These are the people who don't want to explore and wander. They want to skip all the pages and all the layers to find exactly what they want. Their idea of navigation is a search mechanism on your site where they can type in a couple of key words and voilà! Their desired search results appear.

Although this system would not seem to be the most interactive of sorts, the fast and comprehen-sive results provided by your site search engine provides instant gratification for your users. They recognize that they can get exactly what they want with a few keystrokes and feel empowered by this feature on your site. Be sure to review Chapter 2's sidebar, "Building a Search Engine into Your Site," for special considerations in implementing this interactive feature.

SUMMARY

We discussed the specifics of different areas you should check and test in the final stages of designing web site aesthetics. After you add interactive features, be sure to review the checklist again. Each permutation of your site increases the possibility of errors and complications in your site running properly.

You should test for continuity as well as functionality. Remind yourself of your objectives. Are all the elements of the site unified in a specific mes-sage? Is the layout clear? Does the content make sense? How fast is the site? Is it fast enough? Even if you have asked yourself these questions through-out the design process, you need to ask them again and again.

At this point, you may need the help of a user test. You have spent the past few months or weeks developing a site. People unfamiliar with the prod-uct and the subject matter need to see your site to bring in a fresh perspective. People unfamiliar with the web in general need to see your site. The feed-back that you get is valuable information you can apply to future web design projects.

After you conduct your test, you need to weave this feedback about user likes and dislikes into the design of the interface. Remember that each change must reinforce the brand, be consistent with the web aesthetics, and be able to fully engage and empower your users.

CHAPTER 5

AS A WEB SITE DEVELOPER, DESIGNER, PRODUCER, OR MARKETING PERSON, YOU NEVER GO OFF DUTY. AFTER THE WEB SITE IS FINISHED, YOU ARE RESPONSIBLE FOR MAKING SURE THAT PEOPLE ACTUALLY VISIT. YOU NEED TO BE ABLE TO TAKE ADVANTAGE OF ANY OPPORTUNITIES TO PROMOTE YOUR WEB SITE. WHAT GOOD IS A KILLER INTERACTIVE WEB SITE WITHOUT HAVING PEOPLE TO INTERACT WITH IT? THIS CHAPTER HELPS YOU MAXIMIZE THE NUMBER OF VISITORS WHO REACH YOUR SITE.

PROMOTING YOUR WEB SITE

BECAUSE NOT EVERYONE HAS THE BUDGET TO THROW A STAR-STUDDED GALA CELEBRATION OR HIRE SKY WRITERS AND BLIMPS TO LAUNCH THEIR WEB SITE, WE HAVE WRITTEN THIS CHAPTER TO HELP YOU TAKE ADVANTAGE OF AVAILABLE RESOURCES. WE SHOW YOU HOW TO REGISTER YOUR SITE WITH SEARCH ENGINES AND INTERNET DIRECTORIES, HOW TO PUT TOGETHER MEDIA ANNOUNCEMENTS, AS WELL AS HOW TO PREPARE AN EFFECTIVE WEB SITE DEMO. THIS CHAPTER GUIDES YOU THROUGH THE PROCESS OF WORKING WITH YOUR CLIENT AND STRATEGIC PARTNERS TO PROMOTE YOUR SITE SUCCESSFULLY THROUGH SUCH METHODS AS WEB AD BANNERS AND RECIPROCAL LINKS.

LAUNCH YOUR WEB SITE WITH A BANG!

A successful web site launch takes a considerable amount of preparation before the actual launch date. This section marks out what you should do before the launch to ensure that your web site premiere comes off without a hitch. You want to be able to introduce (or reintroduce in the case of a site redesign) your site to the world with a bang and not a whimper. Don't wait for the media to come to you; you must approach the media. You also should evangelize the site within the client company. Take advantage of the sheer numbers within this ready audience and make sure that enough internal promotion happens before the launch. "Think globally and act locally"…first.

PREPARING FOR THE LAUNCH

What better way to drive traffic to your site than to get other people to do it for you free? Internet search engines and directories provide free exposure and therefore traffic to sites on the web. Make sure to take advantage of registering your site in several different relevant categories. The more general-interest your site covers and the less manufacturer-based it is, the more it appeals to a broader, return audience.

After your site is live, you want to make sure people know about it. In addition to offline promotion such as press releases, you should register your site with the major site directories and search engines so that people searching for information related to your site know your site exists.

Although there are literally hundreds of search engines and directories, the most popular are (in no particular order) Yahoo, AltaVista, HotBot, Excite, Lycos, WebCrawler, and InfoSeek. Each of these provides some form of "Add URL" feature (see Figure 5.1), enabling you to add your site to their index. There also are services available, such as Submit It! and WebPromote, that add your site to these and other search engines free or for a small fee.

The following are the top web site directories and search engines, as well as site promotion services:

- AltaVista
  http://www.altavista.digital.com/
- Excite http://www.excite.com/
- HotBot http://www.hotbot.com/
- InfoSeek http://www.infoseek.com/
- Lycos http://www.lycos.com/
- WebCrawler http://www.webcrawler.com/
- Yahoo http://www.yahoo.com/
- Submit-It http://www.submit-it.com/
- WebPromote http://www.webpromote.com/

With the exception of Yahoo, all of the search engines listed are driven by a robot, or spider, which is a program that visits web pages and records information about them into a database. The information they record to describe the page is usually of two forms. Some robots simply grab the title of the page and any text that shows on the page. Other robots use a more sophisticated technique that involves gleaning the description and search keywords for a site embedded in the head of the document using <META> tags. You can use the following syntax to ensure that these robots get an accurate description of your site:

```
<HEAD>
<TITLE>Gadgets, Inc.</TITLE>
<META NAME="description" CONTENT="Gadgets,
Inc. is a professional developer of gadgets
and widgets for many applications. If you
need a widget, Gadgets, Inc. has the widget
for you!">
```

```
<META NAME="keywords" CONTENT="gadgets,wid-
gets,doodads,whatchamacallits,thingam-
abobs">
```

After your site has been indexed using this syntax, any search for the keywords returns the title of your site and the accompanying description in the list of matches.

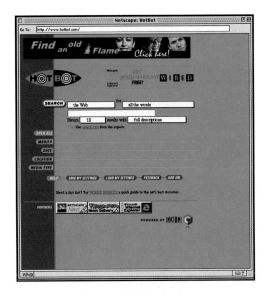

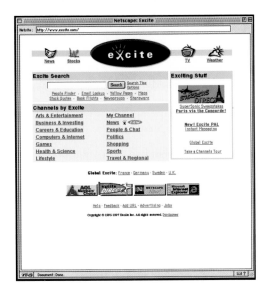

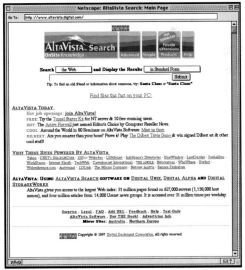

Figure 5.1

The fab four: Yahoo, HotBot, Excite, and DEC's AltaVista.

Your site may not appear at the top of the list, however, or even on the first page of matching sites. Some webmasters use techniques such as repeating certain words multiple times in their keyword list or hiding text on a page using the same color as the background to increase their relevancy to any given search term. This has become something of a heated topic, and these techniques are sometimes referred to as spamdexing. Some of the search engines are taking steps to counter such tactics. InfoSeek, for example, claims that its robot is sensitive to these techniques and actually lowers the relevancy of such sites or even refuses to index them altogether.

You also have the opportunity of being included in the elite "What's Cool" area of these listings. A "Cool" or "Hot!" rating pulls your site up above the sea of other sites in your category (see Figure 5.2).

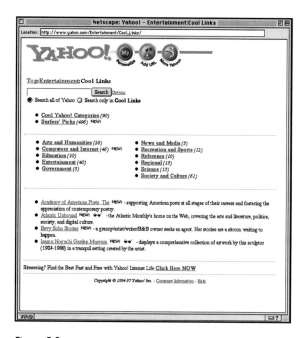
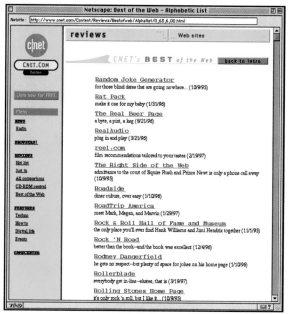

Figure 5.2

In an effort to make the vast offering of sites on the web less overwhelming, leaders such as Yahoo and c\net pick and promote their favorite sites.

ROLLERBLADE: PROMOTING YOUR WEB SITE IN THE MEDIA

The cooler the web site, the easier it is to promote. Working with Cone Communications in Boston as well as pushing a comprehensive promotion campaign within our company landed us spots on USA Today (see Figure 5.3), Electronic Retailer, tv.com, clnet central, clnet online, and Netscape's and Yahoo's Cool Links for the Rollerblade site that we designed.

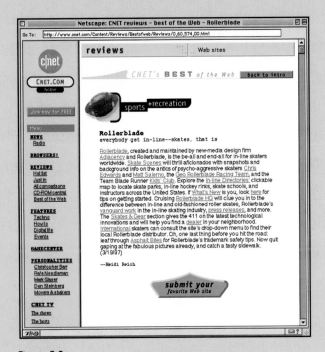

Figure 5.3

Special designations and, when possible, site reviews such as this one by clnet of Rollerblade's web site give you the high visibility and high traffic you need to lead your category online.

When you think of qualities of your site that you should promote, think of the point of view of the user. Help the public relations people understand why your site is a cool thing within the web industry and the product's industry. Come up with a noteworthy features list. In terms of Rollerblade, we wanted people to know that there finally was a comprehensive, exciting inline skating site for all types of inline skaters. We wanted people to know that the web site provided places for people to skate as well as detailed product information concerning upgrades and maintenance. It was important to promote the breadth and depth of the site, to point out how this Rollerblade site distinguishes itself visually and technically.

We recommend trying inexpensive if not free means of promoting your site. When web authorities said that this was a cool site, it helped a lot. This type of exposure as Cool Site of the Day is valuable and free advertising. In another instance we created a site about yeast and because it was deemed cool by Netscape and Yahoo, we gained a tremendous amount of traffic. Directories and search engines are always looking for cool content. After submitting our site, someone at Netscape emailed us right away saying how much he liked our work and asked us to announce to Netscape the next time we launched another site and they would check it out right away. Try these simple types of promotions first before you shell out the cash for more expensive advertising alternatives.

We also ran several generous sweepstakes simultaneously on Rollerblade's site with several hundred prizes (see Figure 5.4). One of the several grand prizes included spending a weekend skating with Chris Edwards, a top aggressive inline skater. Another prize was an inline skating party where a Rollerblade demo van showed up at the winner's house with Rollerblade clothes and skates for the winner and his or her friends. The first 50 kids entering the contest received T-shirts, while the first 2,000 kids received Rollerblade sticker packs.

Figure 5.4

One way to launch your web site with a bang is to run a sweepstakes. One of Rollerblade's prizes was inline skating parties for the winners and a bunch of their friends.

When you do decide to promote your site, be sure that you can deliver and fulfill your promises.

Beyond registering your site with search engines and online directories, a surefire way to promote your web site is by giving demos at high profile industry events and trade shows. Remember that your web site is a product. You need a well-spoken salesperson who communicates the site's features and design qualities to a real life audience. The web site needs to be actively sold through personal interaction with prospective clients and users. A demonstration by an actual person effectively provides an overview and understanding of a web site's offerings. People can see how to use the site and if any questions arise, they can ask right then and receive true personal attention. Keep in mind that a demonstration also includes a regular sales call where you need to interact one on one with a prospective client. The sidebar in this section gives you specific tips on the logistics of preparing for and presenting an effective demo of your site.

PRESENTING AN EFFECTIVE DEMO OF YOUR WEB SITE

Okay, so you built a great web site for your clients. It looks great, it features compelling content, it has great functionality, and your client is so proud of it that they want you to demo the site at the next trade show they're attending. Sounds easy enough, and the parties and receptions should be great fun...with the proper planning ahead of time.

First off, give yourself a lot of time to configure the machine you're demonstrating on or, preferably, bring your own. Bring an emergency boot disk and everything you need to rebuild and configure a system, including the latest browser installer. Bring one of every type of cable and adapter you might need even if—no, especially if—the hardware rental firm says it has everything taken care of. Bring a power extension cord; many trade show venues are rewired for every show and power outlets are a valuable commodity. Assume you may have to plug in up to 50 feet away from your machine.

Try to run as much of the web site as possible locally or, in other words, on the computer's hard drive and not over the Net. Yes, it's faster, but most importantly you won't be as exposed to the whims of the flakiest monster on the planet, the Internet. You need to copy the site to a hard drive or, better yet, CD-ROM, and test every single link and feature. Many server environment optimized interactive features work only on a server, and for those you need to supplement the hard drive site with a web connection to the live site. Be sure to change links to those features on the hard drive copy of the site from relative (based on directory structure) to absolute (based on defined, web URLs).

MEDIA ANNOUNCEMENTS

Work with your client's internal public relations people to write press releases for online media, your client's industry media, and in most cases the general media. You are responsible for giving them all the necessary info to promote your site. You need to be able to advise and tell them what's newsworthy about the site, especially news related to web technology used.

One of the most newsworthy approaches is to look at what your site accomplishes or features that has never been done before, at least within your web site's category. When Adjacency launched Specialized's World Ride Web version 2.0 site, for instance, it featured a comprehensive global mountain biking trails directory to which contributors could add their own favorite rides. Specialized was the first mountain biking-related site to do such a thing on that scale and with that level of user participation and contribution. This feature and others like it were featured prominently in the site launch press releases.

After you exhaust mention of your one-of-a-kind site items, try to objectively determine what your site accomplishes better than its competitors. Land Rover's Outfit Your Land Rover vehicle customizer applet, for instance, accomplishes in a single WYSIWYG, one-page Java interface what many other automotive sites require multiple-page CGI forms to do. That's newsworthy. What innovations have you succeeded at that are more elegant, more user-friendly, or more powerful than what everybody else and their brother has done? Many gymnasts can land vaults, but it's the extra points for difficulty and grace that win competitions.

One of the most valuable things you can do is offer a summary of the site's contents (omitting no-brainers such as "company contact info" and "company backgrounder"). Try to be as specific and descriptive as possible. There is no such thing as simple "product information" in a web site media announcement, only "comprehensive," "technically exhaustive," or "detailed" product information. By including a list of site features, you aid journalists who, thoroughly impressed after checking out a few sections or pages on your site and facing a pressing, perhaps bleak deadline, often simply take your word for the rest of the site and its unbearably fabulous features.

Other areas of newsworthiness include the following:

- Ways a company uses their web site to streamline their business practices
- How a company is positioning their web site within their overall corporate communications plan
- Tactics a company is employing to maintain or push the evolution of their web site
- How high-traffic a site is
- Ways in which a company's web site is opening up global markets for a company
- Anything remarkable concerning e-commerce aspirations or, better yet, successes, and so on

Working with a PR firm also gets you high-exposure spots much more easily. Adjacency scored a full-color shot of the Rollerblade site (see Figure 5.5) in the July 25, 1996 *USA Today* with the quote, "Can web sites get more commercially sophisticated than the new Rollerblade? Graphics are a Wow. And the info is very nicely organized. Inline-racing fans shouldn't miss this." The newspaper coverage also featured a large image of the site menu page with a caption that read, "Inline on line: The Rollerblade site has product information and more, from skating safety tips to a national directory of skate parks." Without the PR person and his contacts, that favorable, national publicity may never have happened.

WORKING WITH YOUR CLIENT TO PROMOTE INTERNALLY

The more the client promotes the site as a destination internally within the company, the more unified and powerful its message is to its audience. The URL or site must be promoted as much as the company's existing corporate communications strategy. Clients have included their URL on their corporate letterhead, business cards, some even on envelopes and mailing labels, product brochures, press releases, retailer packets, magazine and newspaper ads, and so on (see Figure 5.6).

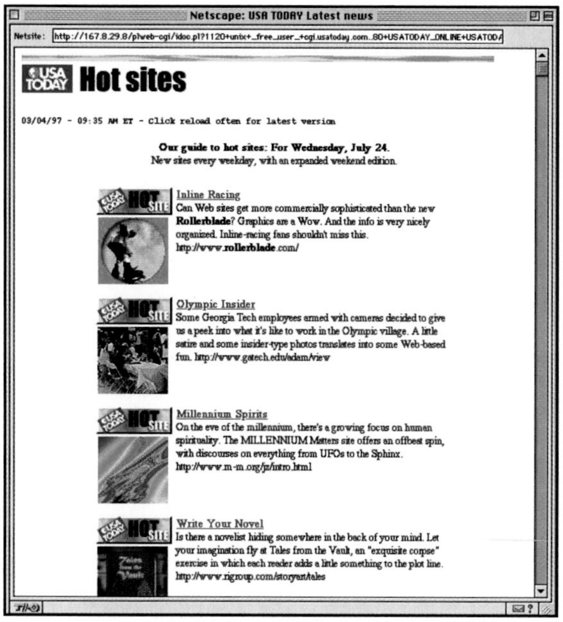

Figure 5.5

Recognition from publications such as USA Today *offer the uniquely powerful combination of simultaneous online and print coverage.*

Figure 5.6

Existing print company newsletters can drive readers to the web site for additional information. Ultimately, the commitment must be the client's. Adjacency's client, PowerBar, is committed.

LUFTHANSA: ONLINE CONTEST DESIGN AND DEVELOPMENT

The biggest challenge in designing a site for Lufthansa was to increase awareness and exposure to an American audience. Lufthansa, a German airline based in Frankfurt, had acquired www.lufthansa.com instead of reserving www.lufthansa.de before any of the people in the American office had begun their web initiative. We ended up having to compromise and choose www.lufthansa-usa.com for the American web site. Unfortunately, this is not the most intuitive URL for Americans to find information about Lufthansa. Additionally, the German site did not offer an immediately identifiable link back to the American site.

We had to create public awareness that Lufthansa had a site for the United States, and we had to create and increase traffic. In order to get people to go to the site and continue to visit over the next months, we came up with a sweepstakes idea.

Lufthansa was very receptive. Airlines run frequent promotions, so they often have extra merchandise at their disposal—Lufthansa-branded Swatch watches, tote bags, coffee mugs, tickets to Europe, and so on (see Figure 5.7).

Figure 5.7

A successful sweepstakes ad banner catches the attention of web users then convinces them to visit your site to register. Adjacency's Lufthansa banners employed a bold look, wit, and a clear call to action to accomplish just that.

We created an entire campaign to promote the sweepstakes that would consequently promote the site. Knowing that the best places to advertise were on the major search engines, we narrowed down our target audience to people interested in things in Europe (see Figure 5.8). Banner ads were created to promote the contest on the international travel sections of Yahoo and AOL. We obviously promoted the sweepstakes on the front page of the site and in the email update system.

People had to return to the site to see if they had won the grand prize that was drawn every two weeks. At the end of every grand prize drawing, users would have to go back and re-enroll. So, if someone was interested, we were guaranteed four returns. On the submission confirmation page, we included new promotions, additions, and information on the site to inspire people to click deeper. This submission form also gave them the option to receive email updates. When you receive these email updates, you get URLs for more info about the content that describes special fares and promotions applicable to the nearest Lufthansa departure location.

By using sweepstakes to achieve product information dissemination and brand identity awareness, we increased site traffic considerably.

Figure 5.8

A good sweepstakes entry form shows the booty first and is as simple as possible for entrants to complete.

LEVERAGING YOUR BRAND OR PRODUCT

As with any other product, whether it's a cheeseburger, running shoe, or car, your web site needs to be advertised in order to reach your audience. This section teaches you how to create effective web ad banners designed to make people click through to your web site. We also go into developing strategic partnerships that build strong, continuing advertising campaigns for your site.

CREATING EFFECTIVE WEB AD BANNERS

In promoting its site, your client may want to place ad banners on sites popular among the users it wants to reach. And the client will likely ask you to create these banners.

So what constitutes an effective ad banner? What draws users' eyes? What makes them click?

Although the ad banner is probably the youngest form of advertising, there has already been research done in determining what makes an ad banner effective. These studies measure a banner's effectiveness in terms of two things:

◆ **Exposures.** The number of times the banner is seen.
◆ **Click-throughs.** The number of times a user is motivated to click the banner in order to view the content it is advertising.

By dividing a banner's click-throughs by its number of exposures, you arrive at a *click-through rate*. This number is the final measure of a banner's effectiveness.

The reports returned by most sites that offer advertising of their pages show click-throughs of 1–5 percent. This means that for every 100 people who see your banner, one to five of them decides to click it. This figure may seem low, but the sites that host your advertising typically don't guarantee click-throughs. You pay for a certain number of exposures, and it's up to you—and your banner—to turn as many of those exposures as possible into click-throughs.

A number of things can be done to increase the efficiency of your banner. Probably the most effective means of increasing user response is to add animation to the banner; this has been shown to increase click-throughs by as much as 30–40 percent. Do not, however, use animation indiscriminately. It can be a powerful tool, but it can also work against you. An animation that cycles too rapidly and blinks too much can scare users away rather than attracting them.

Animation is most effective when used to feed users information in logical pieces that they can more readily understand. In this manner, you can turn your 480×60 pixel banner into a banner ten times as large. If you have a lot of information to fit into a small space, animation is the way to go.

A NeXT advertisement to be placed on HotWired, for example, was restricted to a 125×125-pixel square. This somewhat awkward format forced us to rethink the tactics we had used for banners that were typically long and narrow. By breaking the message up over three frames, with transitions between each frame, we created an effective means of giving the user the information one piece at a time (see Figure 5.9).

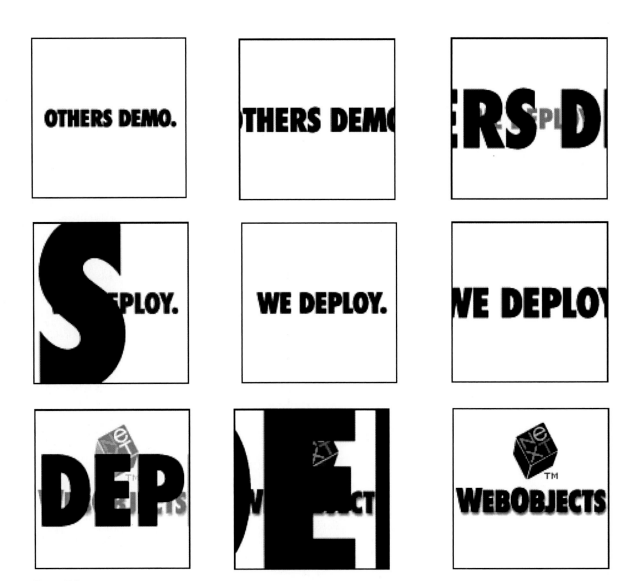

Figure 5.9

Adjacency created this animated NeXT advertisement for placement on the HotWired site. We found the best way to fit the entire message in the rather cramped banner space was to break it up into several frames.

Color is also a factor. Don't use colors that fade into the background. Choose colors that come forward in the context of the page, but avoid using garish color combinations. Help readers to see, but don't make them squint.

If you can add computer-centric appeal to the banner, you can capitalize on the one known quality of your viewers: they are using a computer. The Lufthansa banner that was placed on Yahoo, for example, juxtaposes seeing Europe through a computer monitor with the possibility of seeing it from a window seat on a Lufthansa flight.

Adding an interactive element to your banner is also something to consider. Asking a question in your banner invites viewers who know the answer to click, for example. Believe it or not, it has been shown that just adding the two magic words "click here" can increase click-throughs dramatically.

In a banner advertising Apple's much-touted acquisition of NeXT, Adjacency presented the viewer with a simulated Macintosh dialog box (see

Figure 5.10). On either side of the dialog box was an Apple logo and a NeXT logo. In the middle, a button labeled Merge invited the users to click and witness the events surrounding the merger.

Figure 5.10

Interactivity can be used in an ad banner with humorous effects, as well. In this ad banner created for NeXT, Adjacency invites web users to change the course of the computer industry.

One of the best examples of adding interactivity to a banner ad was an ad for Hewlett-Packard. Instead of using an animated GIF as most ads do, HP chose to use a small Java applet that enabled users to play a version of the classic computer game Pong right in the web page.

Although measuring banner effectiveness is far from being an exact science, these guidelines can help turn your banner ad into an effective tool for generating site traffic.

When you decide to create online banner ads, you need to make sure you are advertising something special about the site to drive traffic. You need to think of ways to entice people to click the banner.

Here is a summary of some content features of an ad banner that make it more clickable:

- **Timely information.** People tend to be interested in new things.
- **Free offer.** Having the word "free" usually piques users' interest.
- **Special contest.** If users realize that clicking the banner could be potentially rewarding, they are more likely to click.

You must also carefully consider your strategy in using online banners.

Where are you going to put them? You may choose to use an Internet directory or search engine. If so, you need to decide whether you advertise on the front page, a specific category or section, or by keyword. Perhaps you want to advertise to visitors at an industry-related site or maybe the web site counterpart to a print publication or television network you frequently place ads and commercials in already.

Figure 5.11

*This Lufthansa ad banner designed for Salon's (*http://www.salonmagazine.com/*) Wanderlust section catches the viewer's attention, then gives them a way to satisfy their curiosity.*

165

How much is it going to cost? What are you getting for your money? The CPM on some general interest sites is less than that at more specialized sites or for more targeted services such as specifying keyword searches with a site such as Yahoo. But very often you get what you pay for. Perhaps your product is so general interest or you're simply trying to build mass market brand awareness that less expensive, less targeted ad placement works for you. The ability to target people searching for a specific term or product on an online search engine, however, is pretty compelling.

What are you going to do with the real estate after you buy it? Some companies concentrate so heavily on ad banner placement that they forget the importance of effective and compelling ad banner writing and design. A banner in the right place at the right time isn't worth much if it doesn't elicit the right response.

CO-PROMOTING YOUR SITE

Partnering with other organizations and companies to promote each other's sites increases the opportunities to drive traffic to your web site. By creating a special interest site together, you create a solutions-oriented site that highlights each of your products and services.

AAA could include an area in its site about travel safety and point out how a cellular phone would help one be prepared in the event of an emergency, for example. After discussing the different issues about travel safety, it can point out that Motorola, let's say, would be an excellent option for fulfilling this need.

Through partnerships, you pool together resources to build a strong client base. Remember what we told you about competition and how every web site is a potential competitor? Well, you can turn this concept around in your favor. From your competitor list, you must be able to identify partnership opportunities. It may not be practical for you to set out to be the one-stop shop for your users, especially when just starting out.

In life, an effective leader does not necessarily need to *have* all of the answers; he or she must simply be able to *find* the answers. You can do the same by providing links on your site to sites that support your products and fundamental message. Imagine how you would feel if you went to a grocery store in a desperate search for a certain type of toilet paper and the clerk told you that they didn't have it in stock, but would order it for you, or better yet, they would call the nearest store to track down some rolls for you? As a consumer, you would be thrilled to have options and to have someone on the other side who was sympathetic with your needs and so willing to help. By taking this kind of approach to customer service and partnering with other sites, you can make your site stronger. This section's case study of the Rollerblade and Kodak co-promotion gives you a better idea of how to establish effective partnerships to drive more traffic to your site and establish a relationship with another company who might be able to help you in future promotions. Guidelines are also provided to help you determine whether or not co-promotions and reciprocal links are, in fact, the right thing for you and your site.

ROLLERBLADE AND KODAK: DOUBLE YOUR EXPOSURE

Promoting a web site can be as easy as leveraging off of another company's promotional efforts for its web site. In the spring of 1997, the Eastman Kodak Company web site came up with the Kodak Fun Saver Cameras Find the Fun Files Website Game. This scavenger hunt and sweepstakes rewarded hundreds of Internet adventurers with spectacular prizes from major co-sponsors for tracking down the missing Fun Files.

Figure 5.12

Online co-promotions are a way several sites can cooperate to supplement each other's traffic. Visitors participating in a recent Kodak web game were sent to web sites such as Rollerbalde.com in search of prizes...

The co-sponsors included Rollerblade, Inc., Bombardier Motor Corporation of America (makers of Ski-Doo snowmobiles and Sea-Doo watercrafts), and Fossil, Inc. (makers of Fossil watches). Participants who completed the game were eligible to win prizes such as Rollerblade Spirit Blade ABT inline skate packages, including skates and protective gear; a Ski-Doo Formula III snowmobile; a Sea-Doo HX personal watercraft; Fossil watches; Kodak Fun Saver duffel bags; and hundred of T-shirts and hats from all of the co-sponsors. The game took players to the other sponsors' sites in order to find the missing Fun Files.

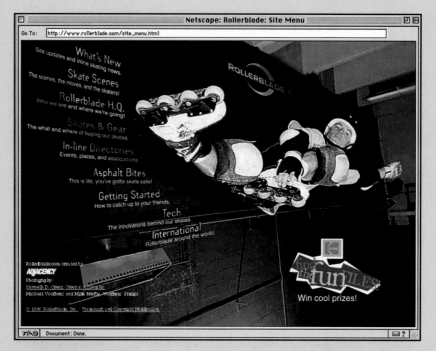

Figure 5.13

...where, in turn, they were invited to visit Kodak to participate in the promotion.

This scavenger hunt became an excellent way for people to become familiar with some cool, fun web sites, while registering to win exciting prizes. If you can participate in an event or promotion with other companies that can offer rewards to its users, you increase your chances of expanding your audience.

Most corporate webmasters of noteworthy, well-designed sites receive countless emails every month from webmasters of other sites requesting links to their sites. Early in the run of any great web site, it helps to develop a link policy. The first question you must determine is whether you want to link to external sites. Many companies decide the last thing they want to do is direct visitors away from their site. Others use links to external sites to supplement their information, offering and reinforcing alliances with strategic partners, rewarding retailers, or rewarding civilians who have done good jobs building related sites.

There are a few key questions you need to consider:

◆ Will you be discriminatory in linking to external sites from your own? If so, what criteria will you use to determine eligibility?
◆ How prominently are you willing to feature links to external sites on your site?
◆ Will you distinguish between different categories of external sites?
◆ What do you get in return?

Companies often fail to ask themselves that last question. Many sites feature a section titled "Links" as a way of filling out the site menu line-up. They believe it's compulsory. Contrary to what some extremely vocal "experts" say, a web site, if it's good enough, can be designed to be a dead end on the web. If, however, you're going to give visitors to your site clearly marked exits, you must do it right.

First, you must keep your links to the outside current. We all experience the disappointment of clicking one of a company's recommended links only to get a "File Not Found" warning. Fair or unfair, it reflects negatively on the site that tried to send you there. Run link-checker programs, have part-timers or bored production people manually click them, and so on. Every three months, you should have somebody in your organization return to the sites to which you're linked to make sure they're still relevant.

If you find related sites worth linking to or webmasters of related sites have requested links, you may want to request a reciprocal link. Simplified, you link to mine, I link to yours. By doing so, you're dropping more lines in the water in places where you know the fish like similar bait to what you have. If you provide sites interested in linking to you with a link badge GIF or a logotype, you're gaining real estate and brand presence elsewhere on the web—for free (see Figure 5.14).

You can also use more tangible exchanges to get links back to your site. Be willing to swap your product for links. If you made other kinds of advertising investments, use your relationship with the companies with which you advertised. Let's say, for example, you spend thousands of dollars for print ads in a certain magazine. When the people there decide to create their own web site one day, be sure that you ask for a link in return for your loyal business.

Always remind yourself that there are ever-present opportunities for promoting your site through the relationships you have and will have with other companies and organizations.

SUMMARY

Remember that your job in promoting your web site is easier if you have a cool and truly interactive web site to promote in the first place. Wow! If you follow the concepts from Chapters 1 through 4, promoting your web site should be a piece of cake! Nonetheless, you must constantly be on the lookout for promotional opportunities. No press is bad press. In addition, the more people you have involved in promoting the site, such as public relation firms and strategic partners, the stronger your advertising campaign will be.

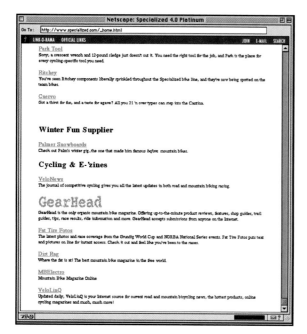
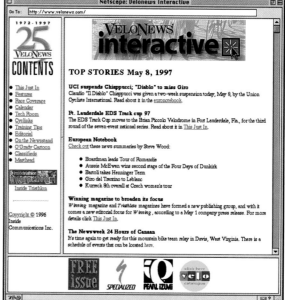

Figure 5.14

Reciprocal links provide a win-win promotion for you and another company. Specialized and VeloNews, for instance, refer visitors with very similar interests to each other's sites.

CHAPTer 6

THE TRUTH BE KNOWN: YOUR WEB SITE WILL NEVER BE FINISHED. DON'T KID YOURSELF INTO THINKING THAT IT EVER IS. THOSE "UNDER CONSTRUCTION" SIGNS THAT YOU MIGHT HAVE USED ON A PAGE IN PROGRESS? TOSS THEM OUT! IN THEORY, WEB SITES ARE ALWAYS IN PROGRESS AND UNDER CONSTRUCTION. PEOPLE ALREADY EXPECT YOU

MAINTAIN IN YOUR WEBSITES

TO UPDATE YOUR SITE AND KEEP YOUR CONTENT CURRENT. IT'S THE WEB AFTER ALL, NOT AN INTERSTATE HIGHWAY. WEB SURFERS DON'T NEED LITTLE ORANGE CODES AND BRIGHT BLINKY SIGNS TO INDICATE CONSTRUCTION AREAS. THERE IS ALWAYS ROOM FOR IMPROVEMENT. WE LIKE TO FOLLOW THE SAYING, "NEVER LEAVE WELL ENOUGH ALONE."

MAINTAINING YOUR WEB SITE STARTS AT THE BEGINNING OF THE DEVELOPMENT PROCESS AND NEVER REALLY ENDS. IT CONTINUES AS YOUR CLIENT'S NEEDS CHANGE AND EVOLVE. IN CHAPTERS 2 THROUGH 4, WE REMINDED YOU TO CONSIDER HOW MUCH TIME AND EFFORT IT WOULD TAKE TO IMPLEMENT AND MAINTAIN ANY SITE DESIGNS, FEATURES, OR ENHANCEMENTS. IN THIS CHAPTER, WE SHOW YOU HOW TO CULTIVATE AN ONGOING DIALOG WITH YOUR CLIENT IN ORDER TO EASE SITE MAINTENANCE, HOW TO KEEP THE TRAFFIC YOU'VE ATTRACTED IN CHAPTER 5, AND HOW TO PLAN FOR PERIODIC SITE REDESIGNS.

KEEP YOUR WEB SITE FRESH

The responsibility of keeping web site content current and updated does not entirely rest on your shoulders. If you keep in close contact with your client, you will be in touch with his or her changing needs. The site you have designed will inspire more people within the client's company to get their content up there, too and your client will primarily drive up the updates. What if your client is creatively challenged? That's what you're there for. You are responsible for returning to each new conversation with your client with new ideas for how you can improve the site. This section delves into the specifics of working with your client and how you should pay close attention to the market and the competition.

MAINTAIN AN ONGOING DIALOG WITH THE CLIENT

When you design a web site for someone, you and your client should decide what role you play in the post-launch life of the web site. When your clients expect you to create the preliminary design and production of the site without any future edits on your part, you should educate them on the best and most efficient ways to maintain the site. It doesn't do much for your portfolio if you simply walk away from a project without providing any input on the future of the site. In this section, we have included a sidebar that describes how to write a "care-and-feeding" manual for your clients.

WRITING A CARE-AND-FEEDING MANUAL

Most clients who come to Adjacency asking us to build a site also expect us to maintain it for them. On occasion, they only want us to do the initial site design and construction. Once the initial phase of development is completed, they bring the site in-house to maintain and serve it themselves. In such cases, we create what is known as a care-and-feeding manual to help the clients understand what we have created and what they need to do to maintain it.

The most extensive example of this was a guide we created for Bicycle Guide, a monthly print publication that wanted to move its magazine online and supplement it with frequent updates. The site includes several different content areas highlighting new stories, with an archive linking to older features. The site also includes a site-wide, full-text search engine that could be used to find any articles containing a certain keyword (see Figure 6.1).

The care-and-feeding guide we created covered several key areas: organizing files, creating new content, archiving old content, updating the home page and section menu pages, managing the site map, working with the search engine, and making new graphics.

The organization of the site was geared specifically to their needs as a content-oriented site. They wanted to feature new content on a near-daily basis, so we created a date-oriented directory structure. For this to work properly, we created a set of guidelines to be followed in creating new content and archiving old content. These procedures were clearly outlined in the care-and-feeding manual (see Figure 6.2).

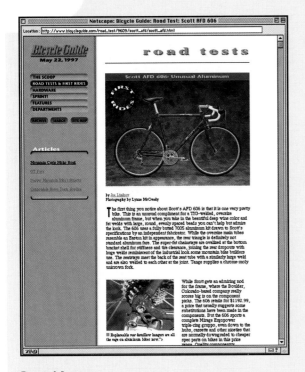

Figure 6.1

A typical page from the Bicycle Guide site Adjacency designed and built for Petersen Publishing.

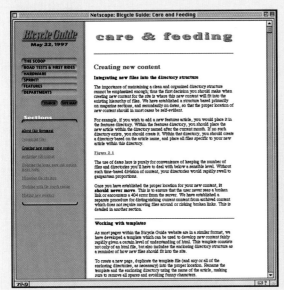

Figure 6.2

To enable the Bicycle Guide staff to maintain their site, Adjacency created a detailed Care and Feeding guide. Here, the reader is instructed on how to create, add, and group new content.

The formats used for the home page and section menu pages relied heavily on tables, so the care-and-feeding manual also clearly explained how to modify these. Similarly, the maintenance of the site map was outlined in the guide.

As the search engine on the site relied on <META> tags in the head of each document, the guide also explained the use of <META> tags and the information they would need to include there.

The last section of the guide explained the standard procedures we had developed for generating graphics for the site, including such details as font faces, font sizes, RGB values, pixel offsets for shadows, and radius values for blurs. All of these instructions were meant to ensure that any new graphics created for the site would match the style of existing graphics.

If you have a client who wants to bring its site in-house, you need to ensure that it has someone on hand who understands the basics of HTML and generating graphics for the web. Then you need to work closely with this person to ensure he or she knows the procedures needed for the proper care and feeding of the site.

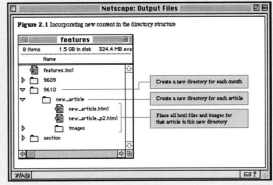

The questions we included in Chapter 1, "Evaluating the Brand," are part of an ongoing dialog we have with our clients. The issues of corporate identity and brand strategy constantly evolve for every company. If your client doesn't have a new strategy or campaign, a competitor may create something that motivates you to come up with something better.

In other cases, you and your client can share an understanding from the start that you are responsible for the web site from concept to completion. In these instances, you should ask your client about their future goals and strategies, even in the planning stages and first draft of the site. We recommend that you review Chapter 1 on evaluating your client's brand as well as Chapter 2 on developing site strategies and structure. The following is a detailed case study about how we have made the Land Rover web site a primary medium for the company's marketing efforts because of our close relationship and constant communication with them about the opportunities of the web.

LAND ROVER: WORKING WITH YOUR CLIENT BEYOND THE LAUNCH

For Land Rover's site (`http://www.landrover.com`), we went live with detailed product information, company background information, industry news, a dealer locator, a literature request module, and an interface with fewer main section icons. We designed the site knowing that it would expand and be updated with more press releases and news stories. We determined early on that we needed to remain in close contact with our client because projects are always in the works and made sure that we were in the loop if and when the public relations department sent out press releases. We knew that this type of timely content would be the best way to keep the site fresh.

We made sure that when the Camel Trophy event was going on in whatever exotic location, there would be a Land Rover contact person onsite who could get updates from people at the event and fax us the information. We then were able to post this content quickly and effectively. Land Rover site users could get the information as if they were at the event! When the event selection process began for the next year in Mongolia (1997 Camel Trophy), we came up with an online application form that visitors could use to try to qualify for the first round of selections. Interestingly enough, one of the people who applied through the web site from the United States made it to the final cut.

Because of our close relationship with our client, we know right away what's on the minds of the people there. Land Rover came to us wanting to promote its "Invitations" mini-off-roading vacations. Beyond providing basic descriptions and contact information for reservations, we made sure that each type of trip had its own individual page. This focus on the program reinforced the ideal of Land Rover ownership as a lifestyle motif—something that a product catalog on its own cannot achieve. When Land Rover was coming out with its clothing, footwear, and accessory lines in the United States, we decided to add a new main section called "Gear" (see Figure 6.3). This exposure on the site was consistent with Land Rover's efforts to promote the merchandise.

Figure 6.3

When Land Rover launched the Land Rover Gear clothing and accessories line, an online product catalog was seamlessly integrated into the site within a week.

Going into the project, we knew that we would have to revamp the vehicle section on a regular basis. With our improved technology for manipulating graphics and handling other technical issues, we could add bigger images to the site. We pulled in what we had learned since the last design and tried to make the site as functional and engaging as possible. At the same time, we knew we couldn't change the look completely. What we did had to be consistent with the brand image and consumer expectations. We changed the design of the individual vehicle section introduction pages, for instance, to feature large, poster-like photos of the individual vehicles in the backcountry, while maintaining the look and feel of the vehicle section we were replacing. This allowed us to further enliven the section while complementing the pages of the site that weren't revised.

The goal in designing a site is to design a visual system that can evolve and grow to encompass new variants and flavors without becoming too disparate.

We presented our Phase 2 proposal, which consisted of eight refinements and updates six months later. We tried to come up with new ideas and features on a semi-annual or as-needed basis. Land Rover was a good client in the way that it appreciated and was receptive to new proposals and new ideas.

In the next round of site revisions, we wanted to add more adventure content. We decided that a great way to reinforce the existing content and promote the rugged, outdoor image of the company was to show in detail what one of the Invitations adventure trips is like through a feature story. We proposed to Land Rover to send two Adjacency members on one of the trips so that we could generate original content. We used the extensive photographs on the six-day trip from Denver to Telluride over tough terrain for sections throughout the site as well as for our special screensavers that we developed (see Figure 6.4).

Figure 6.4

In September, 1996 two Adjacency team members, Andrew Sather and Bernie DeChant, were sent on a 6-day Land Rover driving trip from Denver to Telluride, Colorado. Video and photographic excerpts from the trip were later used to create, among other things, a downloadable screen saver.

We are always talking to Land Rover on an ongoing basis. We tend to give them ideas before the people there require us to execute them. The more you communicate with your client, the less crisis-driven your projects will be. We have known Land Rover long enough that if we need files, we talk directly to the print design house about formats and deliverables. Our technical director talks directly with the literature fulfillment service. We occasionally have summits with Land Rover, print collateral and point of sales people, and the advertising agency in which we sit down to discuss brand strategy and new brand initiatives. Too often companies make the web a secondary medium. We believe that the web developers should be in the primary loop of information since the web can be updated more easily and cheaply.

MONITOR COMPETITORS' SITES

The process for appraising the competitors' online efforts, as discussed in Chapter 1, does not end with version 1 of your client's web site. In order to grow and evolve, a web site must constantly hold up against its competitors. If you strive to create a web site that distinguishes itself as the leader in its category, you must consistently scope out the competition. Look out for changes and trends in the competitors' style or attitude. Figure out where they're becoming stronger and where they're becoming weaker. Anticipate the competition's strategy so your site can come out ahead. Adjacency compiles all of these considerations in quarterly reports to its clients regarding the status of the competitors' sites.

Though the goal should be to stay ahead of the competition of your own volition, many additions to your sites will inevitably be in response to competitors' site additions. The moment one automobile manufacturer introduced 360° QuickTime VR movies of one of their car's interiors, most of their web-savvy competitors matched it. The goal, however, is to make sure you go one step further than the competitor you're trying to outdo. Simply matching their efforts blow for blow is, in effect, playing catch-up. You must surpass. If the Outfit Your Land Rover feature had been CGI-driven instead of the innovative breakthrough we designed, its effectiveness and overall impact would have been greatly reduced.

When Land Rover decided they wanted to build a feature that allowed users to pick and choose vehicle colors and features, we examined how other automotive sites approached the same task. We felt the biggest flaw common to most other approaches, even that of the best existing solution, BMW North America's Build Your Own 328i, was the fact that the process required the user to go through several pages of forms, answering questions along the way. The process was limiting and did not encourage experimentation on the part of the user (see Figure 6.5).

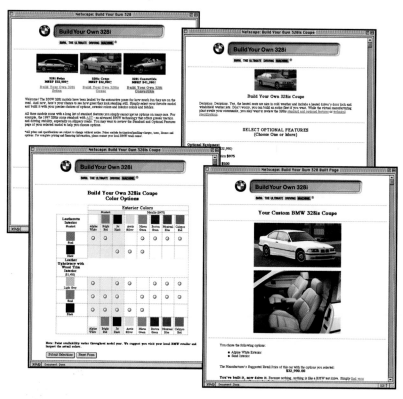

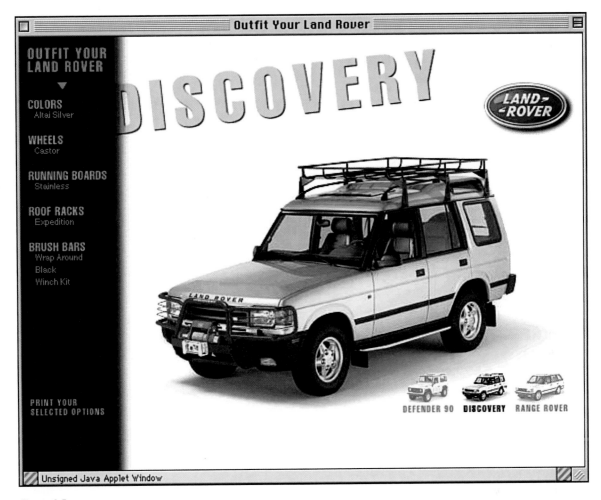

Figure 6.5

By building the Outfit Your Land Rover feature in one window, using Java, we allowed users the freedom to play around, swapping different colors and vehicle kit items as they pleased, with immediate feedback and without reloading the page.

ALWAYS THINK ABOUT YOUR CLIENT

As a web designer working with clients, you never go off duty. While you design and produce your client's site, you are also looking out for the progress in technological developments and how you can apply new technology to the site. Constant brainstorming for ways to improve and strengthen the site also serves as a healthy exercise to keep your creative juices flowing.

When you are not designing or developing your client's site, you are living and breathing the life of a consumer—a consumer who might interact with your client's brand. Away from the office, you are in the context of how normal, everyday people see and potentially use your client's product. You might notice how people move through a store and come up with new ways to approach the interface design. You might watch a movie and get inspired to create an entertaining game or perhaps a serial to make the site more fun and interesting. You might notice some eye-catching billboards at bus stops and think of new ways to promote the site. When you constantly think about your client and remind yourself to step back to look at the bigger picture, you better understand how to package the product in the form of a web site.

The revised PowerBar site and especially the PowerSpot feature are the result of combined user feedback, client ideas, and modifications based on Adjacency employees' experiences.

INCREASING RETURN TRAFFIC

A web site needs a growing audience in order to be successful. How do you make sure that users remain interested beyond the spectacular launch of your new web site or stunning redesign? By making sure that users find reasons to come back again and again. You need to find ways for them to explore other sections and become interested in your site as a whole. You need to motivate visitors to be so impressed by your web site that they recommend others to check it out. This section shows you how to boost return traffic by updating the site frequently, communicating these updates, and developing interactive web features that users can use repeatedly.

UPDATE THE SITE FREQUENTLY

The more your users see and understand that your site content changes often, the more likely they will come back in order to see what has changed. Simple visual clues, such as displaying the current date or rotating graphics on the home page, can indicate to your audience that you have updated and will continue to update the site (see Figure 6.6). The key to this approach, of course, is to make sure you're periodically adding new content, lest you commit the online version of Pepsi's freshness dating mistake. Read the sidebar in this section regarding content freshness dating for a simple method demonstrating your site's timeliness to users.

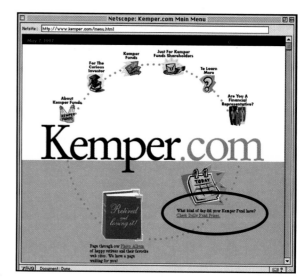

Figure 6.6

Adding dates to your web pages gives users a frame of reference as to how new and fresh your content is.

Because web audiences expect site content to be timely and updated frequently, you should be prepared to provide the latest news and announcements regarding the client and the product (see Figure 6.7). Try to get the content and copy for press releases and announcements as early as possible to prepare the HTML all at once, and then push the relevant pieces live at the appropriate time.

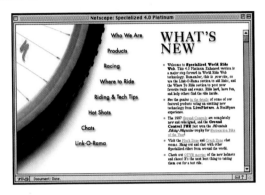

Figure 6.7

When people first visit a web site, they often check out the "What's New" page first. Specialized's web site opens with that content in plain view.

When Rollerblade prepared to roll out their new aggressive in line skating product line, for instance, Adjacency was briefed far in advance. We were given all of the product information and marketing strategy months before the new skates and gear hit the streets. We held the one-of-a-kind final prototypes in our hands. By getting the information so far in advance, we were able to create several product launch teasers to build up to the official launch date. That way, we were able to build the entire launch in advance and roll it out in stages.

USING CONTENT FRESHNESS DATING

On a site that is heavily content-oriented, your users may have trouble determining what is the most recent content. To avoid this, you can use content dating to show explicitly when a feature is posted and when it will be removed. Using content dating also aids in site maintenance, facilitating the task of rotating new content in for older content.

This can be done in two ways. One way is to display a small post-date just below the title of a feature. Alternatively, you can also add an archive date, the date on which the feature will be removed. The other means of using content dating is by hiding the information within the HTML file, within a comment or in the form of a <META> tag. This can be very useful in maintaining the site, as you can set up a script to automatically read in this <META> information on a daily basis, notifying you if the content has expired. If you wish to use content dating in a manner that your viewers can see it, however, you will need to use the former method, or you can also employ both.

One thing to be aware of in expiring old content is the fact that people may have bookmarked that content. For this reason, you don't want to be moving your files around or removing it from your site. If someone follows a bookmark to content that has been moved or removed, they will get a 404 error, file not found.

To avoid this, you *should never actually move old content from its original location.* You merely want to give the appearance that it has expired. To create this illusion for the Bicycle Guide web site, we established a date-based directory structure. Each month, a new directory is created, and new articles are added to this directory, each in its own respective folder. As content expires, the links to it are moved from the home page and/or section menu pages to a separate archive page. The content is never moved. It's important to note, though, that you must indeed update a dated content site regularly, lest you betray to the world your site's freshness problem.

As you may have noticed by now, each of the steps in creating killer interactive web sites are inextricably intertwined with one another. Here, maintenance and promotion go hand in hand. In order to make those most of a well-maintained site, you must make sure that people (a) know that it exists, and (b) know that it is consistently being updated. We like to send out emails to users on a regular basis to let them know what's new on the site. We get their contact information from the feedback forms, registration form, or any type of interactive form where all they would have to do is check a box indicating whether or not they would like to receive future emails on future site updates. See how simple it is in this section's sidebar, "Developing an Email Update Mailing List."

DEVELOPING AN EMAIL UPDATE MAILING LIST

Depending on the nature of your site, you may want to update your past visitors from time to time as changes are made to the site, inviting them to come back. There are certain guidelines you want to follow when doing so.

The most important guideline is that you should never send email to anyone who has not explicitly granted permission to be contacted. On the Lufthansa site, users can fill out a form if they wish to be added to an email update list. A similar form makes it easy for them to remove themselves from the list at any time.

When people sign up for your mailing list, you should ensure that you won't sell their personal information to anyone. In accordance with this, don't send a list of subscribers along with the mailings, and prohibit mailings to the list from any unauthorized senders.

It's also a good idea to ensure that when people join your list, they are notified of how often they can expect to receive updates. Establish a rough schedule and stick to it. Don't email your users too frequently or you risk annoying them.

When you do a mailing, make sure your message is short and to the point. Don't waste your users' time with gratuitous information. Include enough information to pique their interest and include a URL for those who wish to learn more.

You should also be sure to format your mailing list in a way that can be viewed properly using any email client. This generally means using very simple formatting, with clear spacing between paragraphs. You should also wrap your copy at around 70 characters, as some mailers will break your lines awkwardly if you do not.

Finally, you should include clear, simple instructions at the bottom of each mailing explaining how users can remove themselves from the list. Ideally, you should set up a web-based removal form and include the URL in your mailing.

By following these guidelines, you can generate return visits as well as establish an atmosphere of mutual respect between you and your visitors.

You can also implement more impressive but labor-intensive plans to update your site through site redesigns. A site redesign makes a bold statement to your audience about how you are staying on the cutting edge of design and web technology (see Figure 6.8). On a smaller scale, you can also create a special section within your client's site to coincide with a special product launch. This new section serves as an added feature to your client's site.

Special events like contests also entice people to come back to your site if they know it will increase their chances of winning some great prizes. Count down the days until the start of the contest as well as the remaining days during the contest. By clearly specifying the time period for the contest, you can emphasize the urgency for users to visit the site so as not to miss out on the special event or offerings. Treat the introduction of this special event as you would in launching a web site. Make sure that the impact of the contest is as powerful as possible.

USE FEATURES THAT PEOPLE WILL USE REPEATEDLY

In order to keep people coming back to your site, you must furnish them with services and value. They need concrete reasons to return to your site. A user can read a marketing piece once and not need to read it again, but a growing bank of recipes, a growing listing of bike trails, an informative chat room—these are things that people can use and apply to their daily lives (see Figure 6.8).

If, for example, you sell software, providing basic information about your products will not captivate

Figure 6.8

Here, a before and after view of the same page on the PowerBar web site shows a site that is keeping with the company's evolving brand image while employing new technologies (borderless frames and JavaScript rollovers).

visitors for very long. You need to be able to provide a gallery of pieces created by the software and provide demos highlighting the most important features of these applications. You can't just tell. You need to show. Then, you must provide easy ways for people to get in touch with you if they have questions or would like to provide comments through feedback forms.

Through the web site you can also put people in touch with other users. As we mentioned earlier, the more solutions-oriented your site is, the more people use and interact with it. The case studies and sidebars in Chapter 4 discuss how to implement these types of interactive features. We told you how to design effective HTML forms and searchable databases and gave you our PowerBar example of a submission area in order to foster an online community. We want to remind you here that you should think of your web site as an application or tool and not simply a bunch of random pages that can be accessed nonlinearly.

Web users return to sites whose usefulness is not depleted during the first visit. In addition to frequently updated and expanded content, useful or informative interactive features do the job (see Figure 6.9).

To make sure that people continue to find your site useful, you must constantly verify whether different parts of your site work and whether or not they work well enough to support your site objectives. If, for example, no one is sending you email through the feedback forms, find out why. Are people not getting to your site? Are people finding your site, but are not captivated enough to stay very long and comment? Or, is it that people can't find the link to your form? Conduct more user tests. Find someone who has never seen the site and watch him or her navigate through it. Remember that you cannot solve design problems alone in your office, between your cubicle walls, or in the boardroom between upper division decision makers. You need to stay in tune with your users.

Another aspect of maintaining a site in order to maximize its usability is monitoring the quality of the content. Although some issues deal with common sense, such as upholding high standards for the copy as well as graphics, more serious matters involve monitoring content to avoid senseless or even offensive interactions. In this section, we have included a sidebar entitled, "Policing Chat Rooms." Whereas creating an online community through chat rooms and threaded discussions enhances the usability and credibility of your site, an unmonitored discussion area can result in a weak information exchange between users.

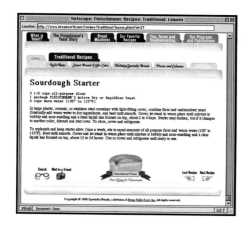

Figure 6.9

The Fleischmann's Yeast web site provides site visitors a periodically expanded bread recipe database which includes a form that allows you to email branded copies of your favorite recipes to friends.

Rollerblade.com hosts several chat rooms on their site dedicated to different inline skating styles and subcultures.

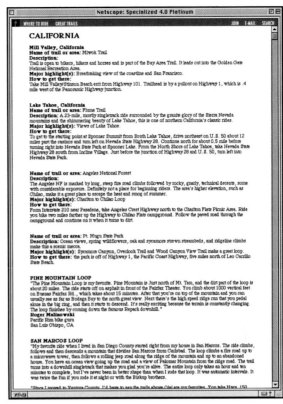

CALIFORNIA

Mill Valley, California
Name of trail or area: Miwok Trail
Description:
Trail is open to bikers, hikers and horses and is part of the Bay Area Trail. It leads out into the Golden Gate National Recreation Area.
Major highlight(s): Breathtaking view of the coastline and San Francisco.
How to get there:
Take Mill Valley/Stinson Beach exit from Highway 101. Trailhead is by a pullout on Highway 1, which is .4 mile west of the Panoramic Highway junction.

Lake Tahoe, California
Name of trail or area: Flume Trail
Description: A 23-mile, mostly singletrack ride surrounded by the granite glory of the Sierra Nevada mountains and the shimmering beauty of Lake Tahoe, this is one of northern California's classic rides.
Major highlight(s): Views of Lake Tahoe.
How to get there:
To get to the starting point at Spooner Summit from South Lake Tahoe, drive northeast on U.S. 50 about 12 miles past the casinos and turn left on Nevada State Highway 28. Continue north for about 0.5 mile before turning right into Nevada State Park at Spooner Lake. From the North Shore of Lake Tahoe, take Nevada State Highway 28 south from Incline Village. Just before the junction of Highway 28 and U.S. 50, turn left into Nevada State Park.

Name of trail or area: Angeles National Forest
Description:
The Angeles NF is marked by long, steep fire road climbs followed by rocky, gnarly, technical decents, some with considerable exposure. Definitely not a place for beginning riders. The area's higher elevation, such as Chilao, make it a great place to escape the heat and smog of summer.
Major highlight(s): Charlton to Chilao Loop
How to get there:
Form Interstate 210 near Pasadena, take Angeles Crest Highway north to the Charlton Flats Picnic Area. Ride you bike two miles farther up the Highway to Chilao Flats campground. Follow the paved road through the campground and continue on it when it turns to dirt.

Name of trail or area: Pt. Mugu State Park
Description: Ocean views, spring wildflowers, oak and sycamore strewn streambeds, and ridgeline climbs make this a scenic mecca.
Major highlight(s): Sycamore Canyon, Overlook Trail and Wood Canyon View Trail make a great loop.
How to get there: the park is off of Highway 1, the Pacific Coast Highway, five miles north of Leo Carrillo State Beach.

PINE MOUNTAIN LOOP
"The Pine Mountain Loop is my favorite. Pine Mountain is just north of Mt. Tam, and the dirt part of the loop is about 20 miles. The ride starts off on asphalt in front of the Fairfax Theater. You climb about 1000 vertical feet on Buenas Fairfax Rd., which takes about 15 minutes. After that you're on top of the mountain and you can usually see as far as Bodega Bay to the north great view. Next there's the high speed ridge run that you pedal alone in the big ring, and then it starts to descend. It's really exciting because the terrain is constantly changing. The loop finishes by coming down the famous Repack downhill."
Roger Malinowski
Pacific Rim bike guru
San Luis Obispo, CA

SAN MARCOS LOOP
"My favorite ride when I lived in San Diego County started right from my house in San Marcos. The ride climbs, follows and then descends a mountain that divides San Marcos from Carlsbad. The loop climbs a fire road up to a microwave tower, then follows a rolling jeep road along the ridge of the mountain and up to an abandoned house. You have an ocean view going up the road and a view of Palomar Mountain from the ridge road. The trail turns into a downhill singletrack that makes you glad you're alive. The entire loop only takes an hour and ten minutes to complete, but I've never been in better shape than when I rode that loop. It was automatic intervals. It was twice the fun if you rode it at night or with the Biskup brothers.

"Since I moved to Ventura County, I'd have to say the trails above Ojai are my favorites. You take Hwy. 150...

Specialized's web site continues to feature constantly growing directories of favorite mountain bike trails and road rides.

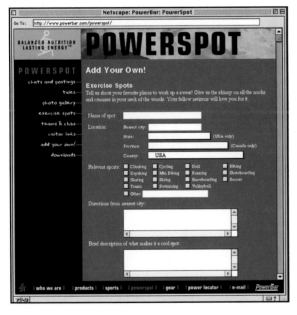

PowerBar.com offers visitors a PowerSpot participatory section and the PowerUser membership program.

POLICING CHAT ROOMS

Chat rooms can be an excellent means of fostering community among visitors to your site. They share common interests; providing a chat room gives them a means of discussing those interests.

Although such a chat room can be a big draw for your site, it can also be a potential source of trouble. When you establish a chat room, you may want to ensure that chat participants don't cross certain lines—or if they do, that you are not held responsible.

The simplest thing you can do is display a disclaimer in a prominent location in the chat area, explaining that you (or your client) is not responsible for anything that transpires during a chat session and that any opinions expressed are those of the individual chat participants, not you or your client. In addition, be sure to publish a set of guidelines for acceptable chat behavior.

In many cases, such guidelines may be all you need, but some situations may call for more aggressive measures—for example, if you want to censor certain words or ensure that your chat software has the capability to filter any such language. Unfortunately, this is a tricky matter, as words with spaces or dashes or other such characters inserted between the letters might make it through such filters, while still appearing readable to the human eye.

Similarly, you may want to filter out any HTML that more savvy chatters might enter into the chat text field. Some chatters use this technique to reference images from elsewhere on the web, making them look as if they are part of your site.

Additionally, some chat software provides a means of displaying the IP address of each user. Seeing this is enough to discourage most people from doing anything undesirable. If they do not follow your guidelines, you can exclude them from the chat on a permanent basis, using IP filtering. Again, this is a feature you should look for in your chat software.

Short of sitting in on every session, these are some of the measures you can take to keep your chat room as you intended it—an environment fostering conversation and community among your site visitors.

PLANNING FOR PERIODIC SITE REDESIGNS

Because you are designing a site that reinforces the brand's image, a web site should be updated just as much as print images and collateral. Take advantage of the fact the web medium makes updates cheaper and easier—your audience will expect you to.

Working on the web enables you to test ideas immediately and exactly. When you have new ideas, execute and implement them. Set up a test area for yourself online or work directly off of your hard drive to see the results in a browser.

CREATE MODULAR AND EASILY UPDATABLE DESIGNS

When building a site, always consider the possibility that solutions you develop in the present may not suffice for problems that arise in the future. These unforeseen problems can potentially make any work you do today worthless tomorrow, necessitating an entire redesign of the site. Such problems usually arise from unexpected client requests: add a new section, remove a section entirely, or move large chunks of content from one section to another. You should not, however, blame your client for these problems. They are merely expressing their needs, and it is your job to meet those needs—indeed, to anticipate them.

To prevent these problems from turning into nightmares, you should build your site with some degree of flexibility, both in its user interface and in the directory structure behind that interface.

The first step toward establishing this flexibility is to determine logical section designations, as discussed in Chapter 2. After these are established, use them as the guideline for developing your interface and your directory structure. The two should closely mirror each other. That is, if your site menu contains six major links, your directory structure should contain six main directories, one for each of these links. If the client wants to remove a section, you remove the link from the site menu and then remove the corresponding directory and all references to it.

If you have a lot of cross-links to that section from other sections, this may be somewhat difficult. Do a site-wide text search for HREFs that point to that directory, and remove these links only after careful examination. You don't want users to stumble upon any errors you might leave behind.

Note the importance of directories in this particular example. Too often we come across sites that have every file in one big directory, with no subdivisions whatsoever. The thought of conducting site-wide text searches on such sites makes one shudder. Don't learn this lesson the hard way. Directories are your friend. You wouldn't expect your users to be able to find the information they wanted if you put all of your content on one big page! Of course not—you divide the content into logical sections so they can decipher it more readily. Do yourself and those working on the project with you this same favor.

In the same way that you design your directory structure to withstand the stress of time and the changes it may bring, you should also develop your user interface with some amount of flexibility. Don't spend hours developing a navigational system with no room to grow. Doing so almost guarantees that your client will come along and ask you to squeeze another GIF into your already crammed navbar.

Taking these steps gives your site a certain degree of modularity and facilitates future updates and changes. This flexibility can save you hours of work and make maintaining your site less of a pain and more of a pleasure (see Figure 6.10).

Figure 6.10

To maximize efficiency, you might consider creating a page and its subsequent replacements in a single batch, then roll-out the redesigned pages over the course of several weeks or months. Shown are several versions of the PowerBar.com opener page based on PowerBar's recent print campaign.

Finally, you can help yourself and your client by developing some kind of easy system that enables them to update the site on their own. The case study in this section discusses how we develop customized client editor tools for each project. A client's public relations department, for example, would be able to enter the text copy, headline, and date for each new press release into a special web editor. The editor tool could, in turn, generate and upload a preformatted web page of the announcement as well as add a link to the "What's New" page or archive list—all at one time! As you will learn from the case study, we develop our own proprietary software that is tailored for each individual project. Available site management tools on the market are quite expensive. If you cannot afford to invest in such tools at the moment, we recommend that you establish basic standard procedures for your client to deliver site content, as discussed in Chapter 2.

CLIENT EDITOR TOOLS: MAKING YOUR SITE MORE MANAGEABLE

The editor tools we have developed enable our clients to make the updating process more efficient. The client provides the content while we create the system for automating the production process and develop the templates to design the layout. In effect, we eliminate any middle people that complicate the process and, thus, the updates become faster and more direct.

Each site, each project, has different needs and different objectives, not to mention different types of content. We can customize these tools per project to provide a service, especially for our clients. We don't use any WYSIWYG editors; we develop our own proprietary tools that provide more control and customization over a project. The users don't need to know anything about HTML and formatting. If they know how to use Netscape and a text editing tool, they can use this system. They simply create an email to type in the copy and attach any necessary digital photos. Then when they submit the information, it goes live on the site in a preformatted layout. They also have the option to preview the content and make any necessary edits (see Figure 6.11). It is a simple system, but we are sure to train clients on how to use it. The system uses the same software that we use when our clients ask us to cover a live, remote event.

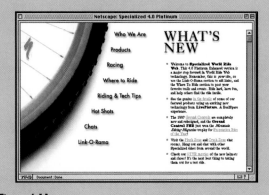
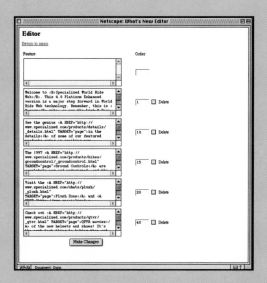

Figure 6.11

Every site has updates—intensive sections that benefit from user-friendly updating software. Specialized.com's What's New content can be edited remotely using a Netscape Navigator-based text editor form.

We initially developed this software to allow clients or Adjacency employees at an event to email updates or results and send digital photos in order to create pages on the fly. With this system, we have been able a few times to beat international and national news organizations in getting news out there to the public.

In general, directory database management can make use of these types of editor tools. Your client will be able to update What's New pages, job listings, event listings or calendars, and FAQs by adding and subtracting elements at will. You empower your clients while you engage your web audience with fresh content.

SUMMARY

A web site manager's work is never done. For a great web site to remain viable, it must grow and evolve visually, editorially, functionally, and technologically. Your site must at a minimum stay abreast of developments in your business. Ideally, you will continually evaluate your site's effectiveness vis-a-vis your business objectives and its usefulness from the point of view of the user.

The true test of a web site is the level of value its users gain from their (hopefully frequent) interaction with it. The moment your web site lags behind any of your other communication efforts it becomes ineffective, perhaps even a liability. Keeping your site modular, easily updatable, well-organized and technologically up-to-date increases the returns on your web investment.

Ultimately, however, the most crucial determinants of your site's initial and continued success is your level of understanding of the web as it evolves and your continued commitment to the project a month, a year, a decade from site launch.

APPENDIX A

TOOLS FOR CREATING KILLER INTERACTIVE WEB SITES

For the most part, Adjacency's production work is done on Macintosh computers, so this tools section has a decidedly Macintosh bent. We have included some tools that we find useful on other platforms, but for the most part this section will benefit you most if you use a Mac.

BBEDIT
BAREBONES SOFTWARE

`http://www.barebones.com/`

Like they say, it doesn't suck. BBEdit is the best text editor there is. Originally created as a tool for programming in more complex languages such as C++, BBEdit has come into its own as an HTML editor. The most recent version sports spiffy tools for automating a lot of HTML drudgery, along with built-in support for complex multi-file searching and replacing using regular expressions. BBEdit has been a staple in the Adjacency diet for a long time and we've found few flaws in it. Try it; you'll like it.

QUICKEYS
CE SOFTWARE

`http://www.cesoft.com/`

If it weren't for QuicKeys, we wouldn't be able to get those precious three hours of sleep each night—we'd still be at our desks, typing `<TABLE BORDER=0 CELLSPACING=0 CELLPADDING=0>`. With QuicKeys, you can throw out table code with a keystroke or two. You can grab colors from Photoshop, convert them to hex, and paste them into your HTML, while you pop open another can of Jolt. It's also possible to switch between apps without touching the application menu. Script the unscriptable and sleep better at night.

GOLIVE CYBERSTUDIO
GOLIVE SYSTEMS, INC.

`http://www.golive.com/`

At Adjacency, we eat WYSIWYG HTML editors for breakfast. We've looked at Adobe PageMill and SiteMill, Microsoft FrontPage, Claris HomePage, and NetObjects Fusion, but none of them seem to stay crispy in milk. Then we had a look at CyberStudio from GoLive Systems. Jaws actually dropped open. I had to wipe the milk off my chin.

CyberStudio is an ambitious product. It's got all the stuff the others claim to have: pixel-level positioning; a customizable HTML tag database; site management and link-checking; WYSIWYG table and frame editing; and direct source manipulation. But GoLive goes way further: built-in support for embedding and previewing plug-in-based content and Java applets; a JavaScript editor and function library with syntax-checking; way-cool drag-linking between files; and an outline editor that is worth the price of admission by itself. Watch this app: future revs promise integration with dynamic content engines such as WebObjects, QuickTime 3.0 support, and a whole lot more.

GIFBUILDER
YVES PIGUET

`http://www.pascal.com/mirrors/gifbuilder/`

The tool of choice for creating GIF animations on a Macintosh. With full drag-and-drop support of most common image formats, as well as QuickTime movies and PICS animations, GifBuilder is a tool that does one thing and does it well. Control frame positioning, interframe delay, and transparency all from one window. Version 0.5 adds built-in effects, some time-saving transitions, and automatic cropping of unneeded image areas. What more could you want for free?

DEBABELIZER
EQUILIBRIUM

`http://www.equil.com/`

Although it could definitely use a facelift, DeBabelizer is a graphics processing power-house. By defining scripts, you can apply (and reapply) a series of commands on a set of files and watch it go. It's possible, for example, to drop a set of graphic links on DeBabelizer and tell it to crop them all to the smallest possible size, index them at 3 bit, make the background color transparent, and save them all as GIFs. It's a pain to learn how to use, but you get more sleep once you do.

GRAPHICCONVERTER
LEMKE SOFTWARE

`http://members.aol.com/lemkesoft/`

For those on a shareware budget, GraphicConverter is the next best thing to DeBabelizer. Although its interface rivals DeBabelizer's in obscurity, you'll find that doing simple things such as splitting a big graphic into

a bunch of little ones is far simpler with GraphicConverter than its more expensive cousin.

ADOBE PHOTOSHOP AND ADOBE ILLUSTRATOR
ADOBE SYSTEMS

`http://www.adobe.com/`

These two programs will save your life. The dynamic duo of image creation, Illustrator and Photoshop are indispensable tools for the serious Web designer. If you can't afford them, ask for them for Christmas. Beg.

SOUNDEDIT PRO
MACROMEDIA

`http://www.macromedia.com/`

If you plan to use sound on a Web page, there are lots of sound editing tools available that span the entire price-performance spectrum. Although SoundEdit Pro is more expensive than some of the shareware alternatives out there, it rivals many more expensive packages in its feature set. With a very intuitive interface, SoundEdit leaves the tech for the technicians and enables the rest of the world to get down to the business of making sound for the Web. It's also pretty good at compressing JPEGs.

GIF CONSTRUCTION SET
ALCHEMY MINDWORKS

http://ftp.north.net/

If you're doing Web site development on Windows, GIF Construction Set makes your life a little better. This GIF animation tool offers most of the same features as GifBuilder to users of the world's most common operating system.

UNIX UTILITIES: BASH, FIND, GREP, AND SO ON
FREE SOFTWARE FOUNDATION

http://www.fsf.org/

Macs are great and all, but when it comes to managing really large Web sites, there is nothing better than a good old shell account. Although the learning curve is steep, it feels really good to change a misspelled word in 3,000 files in about a minute and a half. It makes you smile.

PERL
LARRY WALL AND OTHERS

http://www.perl.com/perl/

Short for Practical Extraction and Reporting Language, Perl is the glue that holds most Web servers together. If you want to use any serious server-side user interaction in order to make your site more dynamic and interactive, learn Perl or become friends with someone who already has.

FIXIMG

This handy little Perl program scans an entire Web site and inserts height and width tags in all the <IMG> tags it finds, resulting in faster page parsing and loading. As image sizes tend to change during site development, we leave them out entirely, and then let fiximg do the work after the site goes live.

PHP/FI

http://www.vex.net/php/

Although JavaScript is great for embedding scripts in HTML, it doesn't scale well across the current crop of browsers and platforms. An alternative is PHP/FI, a server-side scripting language that also resides in your HTML files. Because it runs on the server side of the client-server relationship, you don't have to worry about what browser the user has. PHP is also capable of doing database queries and generating graphics on the fly, things that are difficult or impossible in JavaScript. Because it's embedded in your HTML, you don't have to worry about building and maintaining separate scripts. And because it's simpler than Perl, those whose background is largely in coding HTML will pick it up more easily.

To learn more about these and other great tools for creating killer interactive Web sites, visit the companion book site at http://www.adj.com/killer/.

APPENDIX B

SITES REFERENCED IN THIS BOOK

HTTP://WWW.ADJ.COM/KILLER/

The killer companion site for this killer book!
Here you'll find more info on topics covered in
the book, links to all the great tools we use, and
more.

ADJACENCY'S CLIENTS

FLEISCHMANN'S YEAST

http://www.breadworld.com/

KEMPER FUNDS

http://www.kemper.com/

LAND ROVER NORTH AMERICA

http://www.landrover.com/

LUFTHANSA

http://www.lufthansa-usa.com/

MOTOROLA

http://www.mot.com/

APPLE ENTERPRISE SOFTWARE

(formerly NeXT Sofware)

http://www.next.com/

PATAGONIA

http://www.patagonia.com/

POWERFOOD

http://www.powerbar.com/

ROLLERBLADE

http://www.rollerblade.com/

SPECIALIZED BICYCLE COMPONENTS

http://www.specialized.com/

SEARCH ENGINES

ALTAVISTA

http://www.altavista.digital.com/

EXCITE

http://www.excite.com/

HOTBOT

http://www.hotbot.com/

INFOSEEK

http://www.infoseek.com/

LYCOS

http://www.lycos.com/

WEBCRAWLER

http://www.webcrawler.com/

YAHOO

http://www.yahoo.com/

SITE PROMOTION SERVICES

SUBMIT IT!

http://www.submit-it.com/

WEBPROMOTE

http://www.webpromote.com/

TOOLS AND TUTORIALS

SERVER-SIDE INCLUDES

```
http://hoohoo.ncsa.uiuc.edu/docs/tutori-
als/includes.html
```

CASCADING STYLE SHEETS

```
http://www.w3.org/pub/WWW/TR/REC-CSS1
```

SHOCKWAVE

```
http://www.macromedia.com/shockzone/
```

EXCITE FOR WEB SERVERS

```
http://www.excite.com/navigate/
```

INDEX

204